W9-BTP-532

Coaches Training Manual to

PSYCHING FOR SPORT

Terry Orlick, PhD
University of Ottawa

LEISURE PRESS

Champaign, Illinois

Library of Congress Cataloging-in-Publication Data

Orlick, Terry.
   Coaches training manual to psyching for sport.

   Bibliography: p.
   1. Coaching (Athletics)   2. Sports--Psychological
aspects. I.   Title.
GV711.075 1986   796'.07'7   85-31837
ISBN 0-88011-274-3   (pbk.)

Developmental Editor: Linda Anne Bump
Copy Editor: Olga Murphy
Production Director: Ernie Noa
Typesetter: Theresa Bear
Text Design: Julie Szamocki
Text Layout: Janet Davenport
Cover Photograph: Long-distance runner Pat Porter
                  © 1986 Dave Black
Cover Design: Jack W. Davis
Back Cover Photography: Steve Newman
Printed By: Versa Press

ISBN: 0-88011-274-3
        0-88011-275-1 (set)

Printed in the United States of America

10 9 8 7 6 5 4 3 2

Published by Leisure Press
A Division of Human Kinetics Publishers, Inc.
Box 5076, Champaign, IL 61820

Other Books by Terry Orlick

Every Kid Can Win (1975) with Cal Botterill

The Cooperative Sports and Games Book (1978)

Winning Through Cooperation (1978)

In Pursuit of Excellence (1980)

The 2nd Cooperative Sports and Games Book (1982)

Mental Training for Coaches and Athletes (1982) edited with John
Partington and John Salmela

Sport in Perspective (1982) edited with John Partington and John
Salmela

New Paths to Sport Learning (1982) edited with John Salmela
and John Partington

Psyching for Sport: Mental Training for Athletes (1986)

Psyched: Inner Views of Winning (1986) with John Partington

Acknowledgments

My most sincere appreciation is extended to all of the athletes and coaches who worked with me on an ongoing basis to generate and assess the mental coaching program presented in this book. The program was influenced in a meaningful way by coaches Frank Garner, Currie Chapman, Jack Donohue, Robert Bolduc, Denis Barré, Max Gartner, Jim Reardon, Rob Sleeth, Bonnie Sample, Lorraine Laframboise, and Bob Northrop. The athletes on the Canadian Olympic canoe team, women's alpine ski team, women's speed skating team, and many individual athletes from a variety of other sports greatly contributed to developing this program. Olympic coaches who completed my psychological preparation questionnaire and took part in my seminars on psychological preparation for major events, as well as fellow sport psychologists Willi Railo, Lars-Eric Unestahl, Brent Rushall, and Cal Botterill also influenced the perspective I brought to this program.

Friends and colleagues who provided valuable input on the first draft of this manuscript included John Bales, Penny Werthner, Em Orlick, Brigitte Bittner, John Salmela, and John Partington. Valued editorial assistance was provided by Linda Bump and Rainer Martens from Human Kinetics Publishers. Thank you all for your time, trust, and the unique contributions you made.

C O N T E N T S

Preface

I wrote this book for coaches who are committed to pursuing excellence in sport. Its purpose is to provide a guide for you to assist your athletes in becoming mentally stronger, more self-reliant, and better able to control their own destinies. A step-by-step procedure is outlined to allow you to implement and assess a mental coaching program that I have found to be very successful with high-performance athletes. Although my program was developed to meet the needs of Olympic athletes, many of its procedures are also useful for developing athletes at the high school and university levels.

The procedures included in this manual are accompanied by planning forms that you will distribute and refine with your athletes. It is important to utilize your *Coaches Training Manual to Psyching for Sport* in conjunction with another book entitled *Psyching for Sport: Mental Training for Athletes*, which is designed as the athletes' guide. That book provides specific instructions and examples for athletes to follow in implementing their own plans.

By following the steps outlined in this *Coaches Training Manual* in a conscientious and flexible way and by referring to *Psyching for Sport*, you and your athletes will begin to reap the benefits of a successful mental training program.

CHAPTER 1

Future Psych

I n the past, it was relatively easy for single individuals or countries to dominate a sport because they were often the only one(s) putting a concentrated effort into that sport on the international scene. Once significant numbers of people in a variety of countries began serious, year-round training and competition in a particular sport, that became much more difficult. Skills at the top began to equalize. Today, athletes need more than a high level of concentrated training and intense effort. They must also prepare well psychologically, or they will find it impossible to maintain the lead. To become an outstanding athlete in the future will be even more difficult than it is today. Chemical athletes (those who use drugs) will be either controlled or equalized, leaving four basic *human requirements* for excellence: talent, hard work, simulation, and psych.

Talent. Physical ability and physical potential will continue to be a basic necessity but will not be enough to ensure excellence in the future. Abilities will have to be drawn out more fully through appropriate training and mental preparation for competition.

Hard Work. When discussing the leading Eastern European weight lifters, Canadian Olympian and Commonwealth Champion Terry Hadlow commented, "Their secret is that they work harder." Leading Olympic athletes work incredibly hard to achieve the highest level of performance, regardless of sport or country of origin. The intensity and quality of work for athletes who have broken through to the top of their sport almost always surpasses that of athletes who have not been able to crack that barrier.

In sports in which China leads the world, the volume of work and the repetition of required skills done by the Chinese in training is remarkable. When refining a serve, Chinese table tennis players serve thousands of balls, one after another, taken from immense baskets of balls; and volleyball players will spike hundreds of times in a row. Chinese gymnasts do routine after routine, divers do dive after dive, often for an entire training session. They work extremely *hard* and repeat and repeat and repeat. Equally important, however, is the *quality* of effort and concentration that an athlete carries to the task.

For athletes to train as hard and as well as is required for future excellence, they will need the opportunity and support to train full-time, particularly in the year or two before the Olympic Games. Talent and hard work are necessary, but they are not sufficient conditions to excel.

Simulation. Simulation training, which the Eastern Europeans call model training, is a critical component of preparation for competition. Through this kind of training, coaches attempt to replicate as many competitive conditions or demands as possible in training. The Soviets and East Germans have become very proficient at simulation training. Their athletes are well prepared to meet the competitive conditions they face at major international events because they have been exposed to the numerous possible conditions a thousand times before in training.

A memorable example of simulation training comes from China, a country that also makes extensive use of this kind of preparation. Highly skilled Chinese table tennis players volunteered to train to reproduce the styles of competitors from other countries by learning to play with a western grip. They trained diligently to perfect this style in order to provide ideal simulation training for the national team members. Due to the training time necessary to refine this style of play, those who volunteered to develop the western grip gave up all chances of becoming members of the national team themselves. Largely because of this type of simulation training, China has dominated the world in this sport ever since Rong Guo Tuan became the first Chinese world champion in the 1950s.

An extremely competent Chinese coach, who had coached many world champions, came to Canada to work with our national table tennis team. He commented that compared with Chinese athletes, the Canadian athletes with whom he worked were not as good at taking criticism; they tended not to believe that certain things like repetition and simulation were *required* for good performance in international competition; and they had the luxury of time in learning the physical and mental skills required for competition. For example, if they had not worked on improving their concentration or on really pushing themselves last year, *maybe* they would this year or the next. In China, if you don't do it *now*, many others are ready to take your place. Hard work, repetition of skills, and simulation training are major reasons for China's success in table tennis, as well as for their recent rise to the top in women's diving, men's gymnastics, badminton, and women's volleyball.

The success of the Canadian women's field hockey team in the 1983 World Championships in Malaysia (silver medal) was also largely due to comprehensive and effective simulation training. The team prepared and trained for every known condition, from heat and humidity to annoying hassles such as losing or changing uniforms. Every player carried a change of uniform in a little bag just in case. As it turned out, just before the start of the semifinal game, the opposing team complained that the red color of the Canadians' jerseys was too similar to theirs. Instead of wasting energy on a dispute, the Canadian players simply went to their bags, pulled out white jerseys, and slipped them on. What could have caused a hassle or distraction turned to their advantage. They were prepared and they knew it, as did the opposing team.

The combination of talent, hard work, and good simulation training has produced many champions and will continue to contribute to athletic excellence. However, in the future that will not be enough; refined mental training will be the final prerequisite.

Psych. The countries that now lead the world in sport have been highly proficient in refined simulation training. That, of course, affects the psych because it renders athletes more prepared and allows them to enter competitions feeling more confident. Without this kind of refined simulation training, there would be little chance of rising to the top. To lead in the future, however, athletes will also have to move beyond this point. The introduction and refinement of individualized mental plans will be the final separator.

Simple replication of competitive demands will need to be complemented by the teaching of psychological strategies to meet those competitive demands effectively. Repetition of skills or routines will need to be supported by suggestions about how to focus best to refine the repetition. Simulation, without directing mental focus, assumes that psychological refinement will occur automatically, which is often not the case. Without a mental plan to implement, test, and refine, athletes will not get the most out of simulation training (or competition). To excel, athletes must develop a refined mental plan to be used before, during, and after the event. Without a psych plan and a systematic procedure to refine it, they give away too much. If you fail to provide your athletes with a systematic procedure for refining mental plans, some potentially great performers will never excel. They lose learning opportunities and opportunities to reach potential. You, as a coach, lose many athletes who have the capacity to excel but who have not learned to excel under competitive conditions. To improve, they only need assistance in directing and refining their focus.

An Invitation
to Act

I n recent years the number of books, articles, courses, seminars, and workshops
on sport psychology has blossomed. Interest in psychological skill development
has never been higher, yet there are still few coaches who are
actually introducing programs to develop those skills in athletes.
For the most part, even those coaches who have read the books
and attended the seminars *do not* feel confident enough to introduce
a mental training program on their own.

Almost all coaches recognize the importance of psychological
training in performing successfully. They are enthusiastic about
its potential, but when they put down the book or leave the
seminar, they fail to act. Why? One reason for this inactivity may
be that most people coaching today competed in an era in which
athletes did not systematically develop mental plans or train psychological skills. They have little first-hand experience with training methodology—that is, "how to do it."

Many coaches feel they lack enough detailed knowledge to start
a program. While sport psychologists may think that they are offering a practical and detailed approach, coaches who are seriously
considering it are faced with many questions and uncertainties. The
concept may be as simple and applied as, "positive self-talk and
appropriate focus will enhance performance," but how you teach
that applied concept to athletes is not so simple. Where do you
start? How do you start? How do you choose what is appropriate
for your athletes? What and when and how often do you practice

these skills? How do you refine the skills and provide appropriate feedback? These questions of implementation remain only partially answered in the minds of those who are otherwise ready to act. Coaches are also keenly aware of their lack of experience in transmitting psychological skills, when compared to their refined expertise in teaching technical skills and guiding physical preparation. These uncertainties lead many to think but not to act.

There are also some people who are not completely convinced of the necessity for mental training. "We never did this kind of mental preparation in our day, and we did pretty well. Do our athletes *really* need it?" Although these people may agree that it makes sense to develop psychological skills, they may not view it as essential. In coaching, only those things viewed as essential get attention. True, some present-day athletes may discover a solid psychological plan totally on their own, but it will not happen often or with great consistency. Without an efficient plan for developing and refining psychological skills, most athletes will fall short of their potential much of the time.

Concerns about time can also inhibit action. Coaches and athletes in high-performance programs have some very real time constraints. They want to do what is really useful and what is likely to work, but they do not want to waste time on things that are unlikely to improve their state of mind or performance. Coaches and athletes want to act, and are most likely to act, if they have the *essential* ingredients—"the guts of it," along with a clear procedure for implementation that does not consume too much time.

In the following pages, I will attempt to provide you with the "guts" of psychological skill development, plus enough detail for you to act. I want you to put this book down (not yet!) and feel confident enough to start a program for your athletes. Obviously, I cannot present everything in the realm of sport psychology. I have, however, provided the material I feel is *most essential* for you to help your athletes to become mentally prepared for high-level competition, along with a plan that will allow you to act.

My aim is to move you from the thought phase to the point of action with respect to implementing a mental training program. By putting this program into action, you and your athletes will enjoy the competitive experience more, perform consistently closer to potential, and acquire important mental skills that can be utilized throughout your lives.

Targets and Goals

Jack Donohue, Canada's Olympic basketball coach, tells a story about Susan Nattrass, six-time world champion in trap shooting. He claimed that he could beat her easily in shooting, with one small advantage. She had to be blindfolded. That's ridiculous, some said. How can she hit a target she can't see? That was his point. How can you hit a target you can't see?

Many coaches and athletes have approached the psych in sport much like a blindfolded shooter, with no visible goal, no specific target in mind. Think about it. How can you expect to hit a target you don't have? How can you hope to achieve a goal you have not bothered to clearly define?

In terms of psychological readiness, we often train athletes as if they did not have to enter high-stress competitions. That is why many athletes do not perform to potential in international competitions. If they are expected to compete well, under high-evaluation conditions, they need to practice focusing specifically on mental preparation for those situations.

Few coaches have a specific plan for improving psychological readiness for training or competition. If mental readiness is felt to be an important aspect of performance, then it is logical to establish daily goals with respect to it. You can help your athletes prepare better mentally by setting specific training goals that relate to their competition needs and by helping them discover the kinds of thinking or focus that allow them to perform best under various conditions.

Coach Jack Donohue's training goals include psychological readiness. To help his basketball players mentally prepare he uses the ICE approach: Each player must bring three things into the gym with him every day—*Intensity, Concentration,* and *Enthusiasm.*

Intensity. Come to this practice having decided you will *give it everything you have*—100%—for the duration of practice. Don't hold anything back.

Concentration. When you step on the court, be prepared to leave previous hassles and frustrations behind. Concentrate only on the immediate task. The play before you is all there is. If anything else comes to mind, park it—tree it—put it aside, file it, deal with it later. Have a *plan* to stay on track. Have a *goal* to stay on target.

Enthusiasm. Come to practice with a positive attitude (e.g., "I choose to be here," "I enjoy being here," "I want to be here," "I want to work hard," or "I like being with these people"). Support each other. If someone does something well, tell that person. Practices go best when players not only work hard, but also smile, laugh, joke, and react spontaneously and supportively.

Olympic Preparation

Before the 1984 Olympic Games, I conducted several workshops on psychological preparation for our Olympic coaches. In getting ready for these workshops, I wrote to each coach and asked the following four basic questions:

1. Relative to sport psychology, what do you feel are the most important concerns, problems, or issues that should be addressed at this workshop? Be as specific as possible.
2. What, if anything, would you find helpful in assisting your athletes to prepare psychologically for the Games?
3. Do you feel that you or other coaches at your level would personally gain from learning or refining stress-control strategies for your own use (e.g., to help you cope with Olympic demands or to better serve or relate to your athletes under high-stress conditions)?
4. If so, in what situations would you like to exercise greater self-control? Be as specific as possible.

An overview of the major psychological concerns of our Winter Olympic coaches, who were preparing their athletes to compete in Sarajevo, Yugoslavia, is outlined in Table 2.1. Similar psychological concerns were raised by our Summer Olympic coaches, who were preparing athletes for the Los Angeles games. The major difference for our Summer Olympic coaches was that they were not concerned with preparing for cultural differences; more of them listed team harmony as a major concern.

Table 2.1 Winter Olympic Coaches' Overview of Psychological Concerns

---

Coping With External Evaluation Stressors

- media pressure and hype of Olympics
- expectations of others (Olympic Association, the country, parents, friends, etc.)

Coping With Cultural Differences

- culture shock and subculture shock
- organizational problems and irregularities

Concentration Control—Preevent and Within-Event

- controlling preevent tension
- avoiding or coping with unexpected situations and competitive distractions
- refocusing after setbacks, errors, bad calls

Staying Positive

- maintaining enthusiasm when on the competition circuit
- building belief in capacity to achieve ultimate goal
- staying confident and avoiding negative thinking

Psychological Skills for Coaches

Ninety percent of the coaches felt that stress control strategies for coaches would be helpful when tension mounted, when teams trailed on the scoreboard, when unexpected problems arose, when debriefing athletes after a performance, and when trying to be positive in high-stress conditions.

At one of these psychological preparation workshops, participants (coaches, athletes, and selected sport administrators) first shared this overview of coaches' psychological concerns and then were divided into groups of four or five for small group discussions. Each group addressed one of the following potential problem areas:

1. *Media* pressure, demands, distractions, plans.
2. *Organizational* problems or irregularities, whether created by their "system" or our "system."
3. *Cultural* differences and concerns.
4. *Concentration Control*—preevent and within-event.
5. *Staying positive*—over the season circuit, within the group, and within oneself.

The group members were asked to focus their discussion on the two basic questions that follow:

1. What are some of the specific problems or distractors that are likely to occur in your potential problem area?
2. What specific suggestions can you make for minimizing these distractions (e.g., through avoidance, adequate preparation, or coping strategies)?

This process proved to be very interesting and useful for those involved. It allowed them to share a great deal of experience on some important topics, much of which was integrated into the mental training program that follows.

The First Mental Training Meeting

To give your athletes a procedure for developing psychological skills, I suggest that you set aside time for three mental training meetings early in the season. The specific content for each of these meetings will be outlined in the next three chapters.

Through these meetings, you should be able to stimulate your athletes to act upon what I consider the four most important psychological goals in competitive sport. These goals are as follows:

1. To develop a precompetition plan (to control preevent feelings and focus)
2. To develop a competition focus plan (to control focus within the event)
3. To develop a refocusing plan (to deal constructively with distractions and to turn things around when they start going wrong at any point)
4. To develop a communication plan (to open channels of communication and improve team harmony)

Basic Objectives

The first mental training meeting should be held early in the training camp, preferably within the first couple of days of the team's coming together in the beginning of the season. The four basic objectives for this meeting are

- to set the mental stage,
- to discuss your goals,
- to identify athlete goals, and
- to have athletes reflect upon previous competitions.

To Set the Mental Stage

At the beginning of this meeting, briefly explain why you feel psychological skills are important in your sport. If possible, draw upon specific examples from your experience to illustrate the advantages of mental preparation. Indicate that the refinement of psychological skills will be approached in a systematic way because of its importance for consistent high-level performance.

During this meeting, assume the role of a facilitator, a person who is going to help the athletes refine their own psychological skills rather than provide all the answers. The best mental set for athletes to bring to this meeting is the simple awareness that all of us have room to improve our mental game, coupled with an openness to seek that improvement. If, from the very beginning, coaches and athletes commit themselves to work together toward that improvement, the best results will likely occur.

By guiding athletes through this organized mental training process, you will enable them to develop and improve their psychological skills. They will make many of their own discoveries and will soon begin to better recognize the mental patterns associated with their best and worst performances as well as their own needs for improvement. You will provide them with the necessary forms to stimulate action and the encouragement to act. You will need to continue to encourage athletes to refine their psych plans and goals throughout the year; additionally, whenever possible or useful, you will need to spend time with athletes discussing their progress and concerns.

To make things easier for yourself right from the start, circulate copies of *Psyching for Sport: Mental Training for Athletes* (1986) and *In Pursuit of Excellence* (1980) to your athletes and support personnel. This should be done either before or at the first meeting. The information in the two books will give everyone a clear understanding of where you are going and why. In addition to familiarizing athletes with the basic content of mental training, this reading material will help with motivation and will make the whole process flow more smoothly.

To Discuss Your Goals

This first meeting is a good opportunity for you to discuss your goals for the team this year. Share *your* dream goal. What do you think this team is capable of doing if *everyone* performs to full potential? Point out that this goal is *possible* and that it is within the potential of the people in the room, even though it may not be highly probable. Do dream goals ever become a reality? Did the U.S. Olympic hockey team defeat the Soviet team for the Olympic Gold medal at Lake Placid in 1980? Did the U.S. men's gymnastics team defeat the highly favored Chinese team for the gold medal at the 1984 Summer Olympic Games? Did Bob Beamon break the long jump record by almost 2 ft in the 1968 Olympics? As Israel's former Prime Minister David Ben-Gurion once said, "Anyone who does not believe in miracles is not a realist."

Move on to your realistic performance goal. Based upon the athletes' competitive histories, current motivation, and potential for improvement, share what you feel is a realistic, attainable goal for the team this year. If you have other specific expectations for the team in terms of training, competitions, or psychological skill development, now is a good time to communicate these expectations. It would help to relay the basic expectation that all athletes develop and refine mental plans for precompetition, competition focus, and refocusing and that they fill out Postcompetition Evaluation forms after each competition.

To Identify Athlete's Goals

Distribute the Goals form on page 15 to your athletes. They can write their responses on the form at the meeting.

It is a good idea to talk individually with athletes about their goals—before, during, and after the season. If you have held individual discussions before this meeting, you can still distribute the Goals form. It never hurts for an athlete to reaffirm his or her goals in writing. Once an athlete verbalizes a goal or writes it down in concrete terms, he or she tends to be more committed to it, which is the major purpose of this form.

To Reflect Upon Previous Competitions

Distribute the Competition Reflections form (pp. 17-18) to your athletes. Remind the athletes that their reflections on these questions are important for developing a detailed and constructive precompetition and competition focus plan. Make sure they do not rush through it. We are most interested in discovering the kind of focus that has already worked for them. If there is enough time at the meeting, the Competition Reflections form should be filled out there; if not, it can be returned the next day. Request that all forms be filled out clearly in dark ink so that you can make a readable photocopy for a mental training folder. The athlete can keep the original for his or her own use.

Forms to be Distributed at the First Meeting

Goals Form

The Goals form included on the next page has been used with athletes in a variety of sports and can normally be distributed as is.

Note: Question 6, Focused Psychological Goal, is most appropriate for athletes who already have some experience in mental training and are attempting to refine mental skills. Although less experienced athletes can respond to the question, some may have more difficulty selecting a specific focus area.

Competition Reflections Form

The Competition Reflections form included in this chapter has been used with athletes in a variety of sports and can be distributed without adaptation for most sports (pages 17-18). If your sport is one that requires different terminology, simply adapt this form by substituting more appropriate word(s) for your sport whenever necessary.

Note: In responding to Questions 11 and 12, athletes should state the desired changes or goals in positive, not negative, terms. For

Goals

---

1. Dream Goal (long-term)—What is your long-term dream goal? What is potentially possible in the long term if you stretch all your limits?

2. Dream Goal (this year)—What is your dream goal for this year? What is potentially possible if all your limits are stretched this year?

3. Realistic Performance Goal (this year)—What do you feel is a realistic performance goal that you can achieve this year (based on your present skill level, on your potential for improvement, and on your current motivation)?

4a. Goal of Self-Acceptance—Can you make a commitment to accept yourself and to learn from the experience regardless of whether you achieve your ultimate performance goal this year?

4b. If you do not meet your desired performance goal, to what extent will you still be able to accept yourself as a worthy human being?

Complete self-   0 1 2 3 4 5 6 7 8 9 10   Complete and full
rejection   self-acceptance

5. Can you set an on-site goal of best *effort* (giving everything you have that day) and be satisfied with achieving that single goal?

6. Focused Psychological Goal (this year)—What do you feel is an important goal for you to focus on this year in terms of your psychological preparation or mental control (e.g., a *specific* goal related to psychological readiness for the event, focus control within the event, distraction control, confidence, coping with hassles or setbacks, and improving interpersonal harmony or relationships)?

7. Daily Goal—(A) Set a personal goal for tomorrow's training session. Write down one thing you would like to do, or accomplish, or approach with a special focus or intensity. (B) Can you set a personal goal before going to each training session this year?

8. What do you think you or others could do to increase the harmony among team members this year?

example, instead of saying "*not* get so anxious," "*not* go off the course," "*not* ease up at the end," the goals should be stated as "remain calmer," "stay on the course," and "finish strong." Athletes should be requested to state what they want to *do* rather than what they want to *avoid*.

Summary

By beginning, you have taken the first important step in mental training. At the next meeting, preferably within a day or two, you begin developing a detailed precompetition plan, a competition focus plan, and a refocusing plan. Share this preview with your athletes before closing the meeting.

Request that the athletes read the following chapters in *Psyching for Sport: Mental Training for Athletes:* "Targets and Goals" (Ch. 2), "Mental Plans" (Ch. 3), "Precompetition Plan" (Ch. 4), "Competition Focus Plan" (Ch. 5), "Building Team Harmony" (Ch. 11), and "Communication and Mind Reading" (Ch. 12).

Competition Reflections

These questions are designed to help you reflect upon your personal competitive history and to help you develop or refine a precompetition plan and a competition focus plan.

Knowing your competition self

1. Think of your all-time best performance(s) and respond to the following questions keeping that event(s) in mind:

How did you feel just before that event?

No activation   0 1 2 3 4 5 6 7 8 9 10   Highly activated
(mentally and   (mentally and
physically flat)   physically charged)

Not worried   0 1 2 3 4 5 6 7 8 9 10   Extremely
or scared at all   worried or scared

2. What were you saying to yourself or thinking shortly before the start of the event(s)?

3. How were you focused during the event (i.e., what were you aware of or paying attention to while actively engaged in the performance)?

4. Now think of your worst competitive performance(s) and respond to the following questions keeping that event in mind:

How did you feel just before that event?

No activation   0 1 2 3 4 5 6 7 8 9 10   Highly activated
(mentally and   (mentally and
physically flat)   physically charged)

Not worried   0 1 2 3 4 5 6 7 8 9 10   Extremely
or scared at all   worried or scared

(Cont.)

Competition Reflections (Cont.)

---

5. What were you saying to yourself or thinking shortly before the start of that event?

6. How were you focused during the event (i.e., what were you aware of or paying attention to while actively engaged in the performance)?

7. What were the major differences between your thinking (or feelings) prior to these two performances (i.e., best and worst)?

8. What were the major differences in your focus of attention during these performances (i.e., best and not-so-best)?

9. How would you prefer to feel just before an important performance?

No activation   0 1 2 3 4 5 6 7 8 9 10   Highly activated
(mentally and   (mentally and
physically flat)   physically charged)

10. How would you prefer to focus your attention *during* an important performance?

11. Is there anything you would like to change about the way you approach a competition? or training?

12. Is there anything you would prefer to change about the way the coach approaches you during training or competitions?

The Second Mental Training Meeting

The second mental training meeting should be held no longer than a couple of days after the first, while things are still fresh in people's minds. The three basic objectives for this meeting are

- to discuss team harmony,
- to review a sample precompetition plan, competition focus plan, and refocusing plan, and
- to distribute blank precompetition, competition, and refocusing forms.

Before this meeting, read over the athletes' completed Competition Reflections and Goals Forms. This exercise will provide much information about the aspirations, needs, and psychological performance styles of these athletes and this team. Make a photocopy of these forms; then return the originals to the athletes at this meeting.

Basic Objectives

To Discuss Team Harmony

Before the meeting, read over the chapters on "Building Team Harmony" (Ch. 11) and "Communication and Mind Reading" (Ch. 12) in *Psyching for Sport: Mental Training for Athletes*. Pull out a few of the most important points that are relevant to your situation. Share your views on team harmony: its importance to you, what you expect of the athletes in this regard, and how you think it might be achieved. Set clear expectations for communication and team harmony. Share the athletes' suggestions for team harmony from the Goals form. (I normally list the athletes' suggestions without attaching names to them.) Be sure to allow time to share and discuss both the athletes' and your ideas.

If you feel it would be helpful, follow up your discussion by presenting a simple communication plan, integrating your thoughts, the athletes' thoughts, and some of the thoughts in my books. Consider adopting an after-training reflection procedure for the end of each workout such as the one suggested in chapter 11, "Building Team Harmony" of *Psyching for Sport*.

To Review Sample Plans

In order to help your athletes begin developing their own psych plans, you may wish to highlight a case from chapter 15 of *Psyching for Sport: Mental Training for Athletes* that shows how an athlete's Competition Reflections form can be translated into a precompetition plan, a competition focus plan, and a refocusing plan. Share this plan with your athletes or ask them to review it themselves in *Psyching for Sport*. It should give them some idea of what a completed plan looks like. Review the focus that worked best for the athlete in the case study and point out that every athlete's plan will be somewhat different.

To Distribute Forms

Once your athletes have a good idea of what they are attempting, distribute a Precompetition Planning form, a Competition Focus Planning form, and a Refocusing Planning form to each athlete. Ask them to complete these forms as best they can within the next week and to return them to you. Set a specific time for completion. Remind the athletes to draw upon the elements that created their best performances in the past as reflected in their responses on the Competition Reflections form. Assure them that once they sit down and start filling out the forms, things will start to come together. Distribute additional planning forms once athletes begin to refine their plans.

Request that athletes read the following chapters in *Psyching for Sport:* "Precompetition Refocusing" (Ch.6), "Refocusing at the Event" (Ch. 7), and "Consistency and Confidence" (Ch. 10).

Forms to be Distributed at the Second Meeting

1. Precompetition Plan   A. Content sheet
                                          B. Sequence sheet
2. Competition Focus Plan A. Content sheet
                                          B. On-course Format (if possible)
3. Refocusing Plan   A. Content sheet

If you want to see completed plans from Olympic athletes, consult chapters 4, 5, and 6 in *Psyching for Sport.*

Precompetition Planning Sheets

When devising precompetition plans, athletes should complete both the content sheet (p. 22) and sequence sheet (p. 23), which are provided. These planning sheets can be directly applied to virtually all sports.

Personal Precompetition Plan—Content

Decide what kinds of activities, thoughts, or images you will include in each category below. Draw upon what has worked for your best past performance and upon what you think will be most helpful or most appropriate for the upcoming competition(s).

General physical warm-up	General psychological warm-up	Preevent physical preparation	Preevent psychological preparation

Personal Precompetition Plan—Sequence

Outline your on-site preevent plan as you would like it to occur at the competition site. List activities, self-suggestions, etc., in the order you intend to do them. Draw upon the material you developed for your personal Precompetition Plan—Content Sheet.

General warm-up—physical and mental	"Start" preparation—physical and mental

Competition Focus Planning Sheets

Content Sheets. Three different types of content planning sheets are provided, each of which seemed appropriate for different types of sport. The *Event Focus Plan* (p. 25) has been used for sports such as figure skating, alpine skiing, and gymnastics. The *Race Focus Plan* (p. 26) has been used for sports such as flat water canoe and kayak racing, running, and speed skating. The *Game Focus Plan* (p. 27) has been used for sports like basketball, ice hockey, and water polo.

One of the three Content forms should fit most sports. If none of these forms fit well for your sport, then adapt the form by changing the terminology and the sequencing of thoughts and actions to fit your sport. I have found that athletes can be a great help in adapting these forms to meet the requirements of their sport. On occasions I have brought planning sheets from one sport to a group of athletes in a different sport and asked the athletes to help me revise them. It worked well.

On-Course Format. Where possible, it is a good idea to have athletes graphically illustrate the content of their competition focus plan with an "on-course" or "on-court" format that actually resembles the event in which they compete (pp. 28-29). For a race, this may mean developing a planning sheet that looks like a lane or track or oval. For other sports, it may be putting the plan on a hill, course, court, gym, rink, apparatus, or playing surface. When an "on-course" format is used, it is not necessary to have athletes also complete a Content sheet.

Refocusing Planning Sheet

The following refocusing planning sheet can be used as is for most sports. If some items do not apply to your sport, simply scratch them out and insert other refocusing items that are more relevant to your sport. On the planning sheet the athlete should specify the potential problem and write in what she or he plans to do to get back on track.

Event Focus Plan—Content

General Guide: Decide how *you* want to feel and focus during the event. Then devise a focus plan to allow that to happen. Draw upon what has worked for your best past performances and upon what you feel will work best for the upcoming competition.

Start	First few moves	Remainder of routine program, match, bout, course, event	Last few moves (finish)

Race Focus Plan—Content

General Guide: Decide how you want your race to unfold. Then devise a focus plan to make that happen. Draw upon what has worked for your best past performances and upon what you feel will be most helpful for the upcoming race.

First 5th   Final 5th

Start	Transition	Second 5th	Third 5th	Fourth 5th	Kick point	Final push for finish

Game Focus Plan—Content

General Guide: List the critical situations you are likely to face within the game. Then indicate how you would prefer to respond to each of these situations (e.g., what would be your ideal on-court response?) Draw upon what worked best for previous best performances in that situation. Think of a focus or cue word that will allow you to focus properly to bring on your preferred response.

Critical situation	Preferred response (on court, field, ice)	Focus or cue word to bring on preferred response

Race Focus Plan—On-Course Format
(Paddling)

Outline your race plan as you would like it to occur. Include your cues and focus points at various stages in the race.

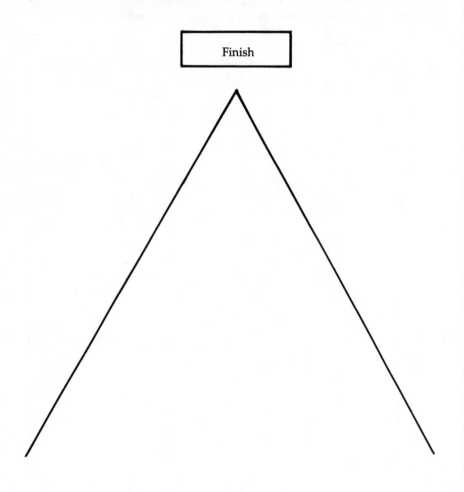

Finish

Event Focus Plan—On-Course Format
(Alpine Skiing)

Start Area	First few gates	Course	Last few gates finish

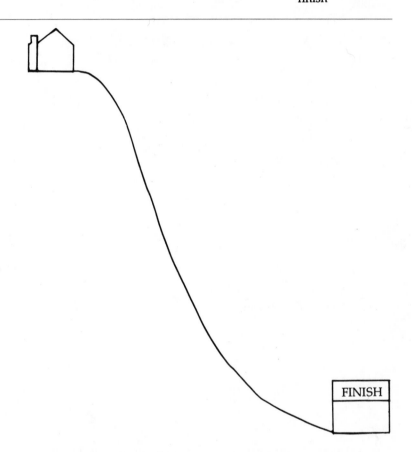

Refocusing Plan

Preevent hassle

Non-ideal conditions

Delay in start

Poor start

Loss of ideal focus in event

Mistake in event

Poor performance (first run, routine, period, event, half, inning)

Poor overall performance (in the event or game)

Other areas

The Third Mental Training Meeting

The third mental training meeting should be held within a week or so after the second for continuity. The four basic objectives for this meeting are

- to return the athletes' completed planning sheets,
- to set the stage for practicing the plans,
- to distribute the Postcompetition Evaluation forms, and
- to set the stage for refining psych plans.

Before this meeting, collect, read, and make copies of the athletes' completed precompetition plans, competition focus plans, and refocusing plans. Also, preview the Competition Evaluation form(s) (Forms A & B).

Basic Objectives

To Return the Planning Sheets

Return the athletes' precompetition, competition focus, and refocusing plans. Point out that they have taken the biggest step—starting. Practice and refinement are now most important.

If you have something constructive to suggest for a particular athlete's consideration, make your suggestion in an individual meeting or make the suggestion in a note on his or her form.

To Set the Stage for Practice

There is a difference between having a plan and being able to implement it. Devising a good plan requires thought and reflection. Implementing it requires action. Athletes need to learn their plan, practice it, try it in simulated competitions, try it in real competitions, and evaluate it. This process will, in turn, lead to modifications and to an improved plan that must be continually practiced, tested, and revised.

Set the stage for practicing (a) the precompetition psychological plans, (b) the plan for focusing appropriately within the event, and (c) the plan for refocusing when caught by distractions. You can do this by pointing out the importance of each plan in pursuing competitive excellence, by asking athletes to take personal responsibility for practicing and refining their psych plans, and by setting goals for mental practice to occur before and during certain training sessions.

To Distribute the Evaluation Forms

Distribute a copy of the Postcompetition Evaluation form to each athlete. Go over the form to make sure that everyone clearly understands what is being requested. Begin with the longer form (Form A on pp. 38-42), which is more detailed, in order to draw out mental patterns. Once the athlete is familiar with his or her own mental patterns and with the competition evaluation process, he or she can shift to the short evaluation form (Form B on pp. 43-45). If an athlete has a clear preference for one of the forms, let him or her use that form.

The purpose of the forms is to ensure that athletes begin evaluating the critical mental parts of their game. The forms will begin the process, after which athletes should be free to individualize the evaluation forms or to tie the key mental components into their own postcompetition diary reflections.

To Set the Stage for Refining Psych Plans

One of the most useful things that athletes can do to refine their psych plans, especially the first year, is to fill in the Competition Evaluation forms after time trials, simulated competitions, practice meets, important scrimmages, and competitions. The questions themselves serve as a reminder of what the athlete should and should not be doing. The responses to the questions allow athletes to gain valuable insight from every competitive experience, regardless of the performance outcome. Through continuous use of these forms (and subsequent self-evaluation), athletes will become much more aware of the kinds of thoughts, images, and focus that help or hinder their performance.

This information can be extremely valuable in helping athletes to clearly understand how best to focus under different conditions and how best to refine the precompetition and competition plan. When this information is acted upon, it will, in turn, improve mental focus, performance, and satisfaction.

Make sure that athletes complete these evaluation forms after every major event. Express this expectation at this meeting, and explain its importance. Devise a plan for the regular distribution and collection of the forms at competitions. The best time for doing this is after the event when team members are alone (or together as a group). For example, make the forms available in the team room after the competition or put them on the edge of the table in the dining room to be completed before eating the postgame meal. But, remember, if time to complete the forms is not preplanned it probably won't happen.

If certain athletes resist filling out evaluation forms, consider alternate means of achieving the same objective. Some athletes may prefer to include their postcompetition evaluations in their diaries. This is an acceptable option as long as they include comments about their *mental state* (e.g., feelings and focus) and how it seemed to affect performance. Athletes who prefer to use their diaries should be sure to include reflections on what they consider the most important questions listed on the Postcompetition Evaluation forms.

Some athletes do not like written evaluations of any sort, but are happy to talk about their experiences and reflections. For this kind of athlete, a conversation following an event is a good choice.

Often it is best accomplished in the evening after the competition. In that case, you can simply talk through the questions, letting the athlete respond verbally. You may choose to write down important responses either on the form or in a diary, as a future reference point. In these brief one-on-one meetings, concentrate on helping the athlete reflect upon his self-talk, feelings, and focus, and upon how they influenced performance for better or worse. Keep things constructive. The important thing is to help the athlete draw the positive lessons out of the experience.

If possible, you or one of your trusted assistants should sit down with individual athletes at the end of every 3- or 4-week period during the competitive season to go over their evaluation forms with them. At this time all forms completed as of that date can be reviewed, and together you and the athlete can attempt to pinpoint the important lessons. This discussion may also serve to reinforce the value of self-evaluation after each competition.

If frequent individual meetings are not possible, encourage athletes to go over their completed forms (or diaries) on their own after every three or four competitions or at quarterly points during the season. This periodic review will help athletes to get the greatest benefit from their competition reflections. They will be able to make direct comparisons between different competitions, helping to ensure that the valuable information contained in that "pile of forms" is acted upon.

Forms To Be Distributed at the Third Meeting

1. Competition Evaluation form

   - Form A (long form)—for athletes in first year of organized mental training program
   - Form B (short form)—for athletes in subsequent years of mental training program

2. Mental Preparation Checklist

Request that your athletes read "Implementing the Plan" (Ch. 8) and "Assessing the Plan" (Ch. 9) in *Psyching for Sport*. These chapters will reinforce the importance of ongoing evaluation.

Competition Evaluation Forms

The evaluation forms that I have provided on pages 38-45 should be applicable to most sports in the format in which they are presented, with the possible exception of Question 7 on Form A (long form). This question is intended to help athletes evaluate each major segment of their performance so they will be in a better position to know which segment to focus upon for improvement. I have attempted to phrase *this question* so that it will apply to a variety of sports. However, it may be of more value if it is sport-specific. As an example, for racing events in track, speed skating, and canoeing, the question could be phrased as follows:

Rate your overall feeling of effectiveness during the different segments of your prerace preparation and race. Use a scale from 0 to 10, in which 10 is "going great" (right on target), 0 is the "absolute pits" (right off target) and 5 is somewhere in between.

30 to 60 min before race   On the way to   Moments before gun
                               starting line

Rating _____   Rating _____   Rating _____

                                            Remainer of first
Start   Transition   5th   Second 5th

Rating _____   Rating _____   Rating _____   Rating _____

Halfway through   Fourth 5th   Kick point   Finish
Third 5th

Rating _____   Rating _____   Rating _____   Rating _____

Comments:

For alpine skiing the question could be phrased as follows:

Rate your overall feeling of effectiveness during the different segments of your prerace preparation and race. Use a scale from 0 to 10, in which 10 is "going great" (right on target), 0 is the "absolute pits" (right off target) and 5 is somewhere in between.

30 to 90 min before race (warm-up)   Rating _____
Warm-up in start area   Rating _____
Moments before your start   Rating _____

(Cont.)

Start rating (explosion and first few
   gates)   Rating _____
Course rating (focus on way down)   Rating _____
Finish rating (as per event)   Rating _____

Comments:

For team sports, the segments usually include general warm-up, immediate pregame warm-up, start, 1st quarter, 2nd quarter, 3rd quarter, 4th quarter, offense, defense, and any critical situations that are normally faced within that game, such as the time immediately following a goal scored against your team. Look over Question 7, and if you feel it would be helpful, adapt the basic response segments to better fit your sport.

In some cases coaches have also added a question or two to this competition evaluation form. For example, in alpine skiing we added the following questions:

- Did you feel confident that you knew the course well enough to race without holding back (e.g., as a result of course inspection and imagery)?

No confidence in 0 1 2 3 4 5 6 7 8 9 10 Complete confidence
knowledge of   in knowledge of
course   course—enough to
                                             race without
                                             holding back

- How much did you search for speed, let it go, carry speed, let the ski go during the race?

Not at all   0 1 2 3 4 5 6 7 8 9 10   To the limit

In canoe racing we added a different question:

- Were you able to fully extend yourself during the last 1/5 of race (i.e., from kick point to finish line)?

Did not extend 0 1 2 3 4 5 6 7 8 9 10 Completely extended
myself   myself (to the limit)

Mental Preparation Checklist

A Mental Preparation Checklist applicable to all sports has been included on pages 46-47. It gives an overview of the many facets of mental training that can be developed and refined by high-performance athletes and coaches in 2 or 3 years. An athlete or coach who wants to be fully prepared psychologically should develop skills and plans in all of these areas during her or his years of active competition.

The form itself, which can be handed out at the conclusion of the third meeting, will allow athletes to immediately begin checking off items that have been completed (e.g., the Goals form and Competitive Reflections form) and started (e.g., precompetition plan, competition focus plan, and refocusing plan). As other areas are addressed, the starting date, completion date, and dates when the plans are first implemented, comfortable, and consistent can be recorded. A periodic review of this checklist by the athlete, coach, or sport psychologist will give some indication of the progress made on mental training over a certain time interval.

You should consider this checklist as a tool for developing your athletes' mental skills, coping strategies, and overall performance. It can also be a valuable asset in your own psychological skill development.

Competition Evaluation Form A

Name: _____   Event: _____

Date: _____   Results: _____

Site: _____   Your Placing: _____

Complete this form as soon as possible or feasible after the completion of each event.

1. How did you feel about your performance in this event?

2. Did you have a performance outcome goal (or result goal) for this event? If so, what was it?

   To what extent did you achieve this outcome goal?

   Did not achieve   0 1 2 3 4 5 6 7 8 9 10   Achieved goal
   goal at all   completely

3. What was your on-site focus goal for this event (e.g., what was the focus you wanted to carry into this event, the one that you felt would likely give your best result)?

   To what degree did you achieve this on-site focus goal?

   Did not achieve   0 1 2 3 4 5 6 7 8 9 10   Achieved goal
   goal at all   completely

(Cont.)

Competition Evaluation Form A (Cont.)

4. Circle your feelings going into this event.

Goal Determination

No determin-   0 1 2 3 4 5 6 7 8 9 10   Completely
ation   determined to
                                              achieve goal

Activation

No physical   0 1 2 3 4 5 6 7 8 9 10   Highly phys-
activation (flat)   ically
                                          activated
                                          (charged)

Worry

No worries or   0 1 2 3 4 5 6 7 8 9 10   Extremely
fears   worried,
                                        scared, or
                                        afraid

Control

Completely out   0 1 2 3 4 5 6 7 8 9 10   In complete
of control   control

Uptight

Mentally calm   0 1 2 3 4 5 6 7 8 9 10   Mentally
                                        uptight

Focused On Task

No task focus   0 1 2 3 4 5 6 7 8 9 10   Complete
                                        task focus

Commitment To Push (Limit)

No commit-   0 1 2 3 4 5 6 7 8 9 10   Complete
ment to fully   commitment
extend myself   to fully ex-
                                        tend myself

Confidence in Physical
Preparation

No confidence   0 1 2 3 4 5 6 7 8 9 10   Complete
in my physical   confidence in
preparation   my physical
(doubts   preparation

(Cont.)

Competition Evaluation Form A (Cont.)

Confidence in Psych
Preparation

| No confidence in my mental preparation | 0 1 2 3 4 5 6 7 8 9 10 | Complete confidence in my mental preparation |

Confidence in Abilities

| No confidence in my abilities (to achieve goal) | 0 1 2 3 4 5 6 7 8 9 10 | Complete confidence in my abilities (to achieve goal) |

Risk Taking

| Not willing to take necessary risks | 0 1 2 3 4 5 6 7 8 9 10 | Willing to take necessary risks |

5. Did you follow a previously practiced *precompetition plan* (e.g., specific preevent warm-up, positive self-talk)?

_____ Yes   _____ No, not at all   _____ partly

If partly, which parts were followed and which not followed?

6. What were you saying to yourself (or thinking) *immediately before* the start of the event?

7. Were you able to follow your preplanned *competition focus plan?*

_____Yes   _____ No, not at all   _____partly

If partly, which parts were followed and not followed?

8. Rate your overall feeling of effectiveness at the competition site and during the different segments of your preevent preparation and perfor-

(Cont.)

Competition Evaluation Form A (Cont.)

mance. Use a scale from 0 to 10 where 10 is "going great" (right on target), 0 is the "absolute pits" (right off target) and 5 is somewhere in between.

30-60 min. before event (general warm-up)	Warm-up before start	Moments before you start
Rating _____	Rating _____	Rating _____
Start	Event	Finish
Rating _____	Rating _____	Rating _____

9. Were you able to fully extend yourself to the limit during the event? (Did you draw from the well)?

Extend limits

Did not extend myself at all   0 1 2 3 4 5 6 7 8 9 10   Completely extended myself (to the limit)

10. What were you saying to yourself or focused on to extend to the limits? (or to try to extend limits?)

11. During the event did your focus of attention stay on your performance (following event focus plan) or drift to other things?

Event focus

Drifting most of the time   0 1 2 3 4 5 6 7 8 9 10   Completely focused, absorbed in performance (following event plan)

12. When you were going best, where was your focus?

13. If you were going less well in parts, where was your focus?

(Cont.)

Competition Evaluation Form A (Cont.)

14. Did you have to make a recovery to get back "on track" during the event? (or before the competition?) If so, were you able to recover and focus again quickly? If you used a "cue word" to refocus, did it work?

15. Did *anything* unforeseen or unexpected happen (or anyone say anything to you) either before or during the event that may have had an impact on your performance (for better or for worse)?

16. Should anything be changed or adapted for the next competition?

Competition Evaluation—Form B

Name: _____   Event: _____

Date: _____   Results: _____

Event/Site: _____   Your Placing: _____

1. Did you have a performance outcome goal for this event?

2. If so, to what degree did you achieve this performance outcome goal?

Did not achieve goal at all	0 1 2 3 4 5 6 7 8 9 10	Achieved goal completely

3. What was your on-site goal(s) for this event (e.g., what focus did you want to carry into this event)?

4. To what degree did you achieve this on-site focus goal(s)?

Did not achieve goal at all	0 1 2 3 4 5 6 7 8 9 10	Achieved goal completely

5. Circle your feeling *going into this competition.*

No determination	0 1 2 3 4 5 6 7 8 9 10	Completely determined
No confidence	0 1 2 3 4 5 6 7 8 9 10	Completely confident
No worries	0 1 2 3 4 5 6 7 8 9 10	Very worried
No physical activation (flat)	0 1 2 3 4 5 6 7 8 9 10	Highly physically activated (positively charged)

6. How did your precompetition plan go?

Terrible	0 1 2 3 4 5 6 7 8 9 10	Felt really good

Were you feeling the way you wanted to feel?

(Cont.)

Competition Evaluation Form B (Cont.)

7. What were your thoughts as you approached the start of the event?

8. How did your competition plan focus go?

Went poorly/lack of focus/off plan	0 1 2 3 4 5 6 7 8 9 10	Went really well/com- pletely focused/ followed plan

Comments (e.g., What was on, what was off, what needs work or adjustment?)

9. When you were going best, where was your focus?

10. Were you able to fully extend yourself during the event (how much did you push)?

Did not extend myself at all	0 1 2 3 4 5 6 7 8 9 10	Completely extended my- self (to the limit)

11. Did you have occasion to draw upon a *refocusing plan* at any time for this competition (before, during, or after)?

Yes _____   No _____

If Yes, comment briefly (e.g., were you able to call upon plan, did it work?)

(Cont.)

Competition Evaluation Form B (Cont.)

12. Did you experience any communication or interpersonal problems surrounding this event

Yes _____   No_____

If so comment briefly (i.e., What was the problem and were you able to deal with it adequately?).

Mental Preparation Checklist

Name _____   Sport/Event _____

Indicate the date on which you:

Items	Started form or plan	Completed form or plan	First acted upon or implemented plan	First felt comfortable with implementing plan in real situation	Could consistently and effectively implement plan
Goals form					
Competitive reflections form					
Daily training goals					
Precompetition plan					
Competition focus plan					
Refocusing plan (preevent)					
Refocusing plan (within event)					

Refocusing plan (after event)				
Competition simulation plan				
Postcompetition evaluation				
Plan for cultural differences				
Communication plan				
Media plan				
Activation plan				
Relaxation plan				
Imagery training				
Retirement plan				
Other areas (list below)				

Meeting Individual Needs

I f you as a coach have some doubts about your ability to develop appropriate plans, remember—you just have to set up the process. You don't actually develop the plans. You do not know the best content for each athlete's plan, nor do I. Our major task is to help athletes develop and refine their own plans.

Are athletes capable of completing their own plans? My answer is an emphatic YES! If they have attended the mental training meetings and have done the assigned readings, they can come up with a plan. The plan may not always be complete or highly refined, but it will always be a good starting point. If they use the Competition Evaluation forms on a regular basis, they will be in a good position to refine their initial plans so that they really work. You can help them along their paths by responding to their individual needs.

Helping Athletes Complete Their Plans

In my view, the most important things you can do to help your athletes prepare psychologically for competition are (a) to make sure they fill out the initial planning sheets and (b) to make sure they complete the Competition Evaluation forms. Then they will understand how to best refine their plan.

The women's national speed skating team was the team that I saw make the fastest progress on mental preparation and enhanced self-confidence. Within the first few competitions of the first year of their mental training program, three quarters of the team had all-time personal best performances. In some cases, athletes experienced consecutive personal bests from race to race. A large part of their rapid progress was related to the coaches' follow-up work on their mental plans.

Before the first time trial, all athletes had developed a prerace plan and race plan for each event, as well as a refocusing plan. After attempting to implement their plans in this time trial, the athletes were asked to complete a race evaluation form. The coach distributed evaluation forms 10 to 15 minutes after each event was completed. This process was repeated after every subsequent selection race or competition.

Between the first time trial and the first race, the coach sat down individually with the eight athletes and went over their plans with them. In evaluating the prerace plan, he wanted to make sure that the final 1-1/2 to 2 hours before the race were filled. If something general was written on the plan, such as "warm up for 20 minutes," he asked what they were going to do, *specifically*. He asked them to talk through their race plan and also reviewed their refocusing plan. In some cases he added a few previously unaddressed situations that might require a backup procedure or refocusing strategy; for example, What will you do in warm-up if your skates are not sharpened well or if you break a lace? He also asked the athletes what *he* should do during their warm-up, before their race, during their race, and after their race to help them. Based on this feedback and his own preferences, he developed prerace and race plans for himself.

I spoke with each of these athletes and went over their race evaluation forms with them after they had completed seven or eight races. That is something you should attempt to do with each of your athletes at least twice a year. Every athlete had made some very important discoveries about how to focus to race best. They had revised their initial precompetition and competition plans based upon their postrace reflections. When you look over seven or eight race evaluation forms at once, the differences in mental patterns for best and worst performances usually jump right out at you. By this point, most of the athlete's basic prerace and race plans were solid and working well. Their greatest need was to improve their ability to refocus in the face of major distractions, a skill I encouraged them to begin developing.

Interestingly, even the athletes who had been competing for many years had never before recognized their mental patterns so clearly. They had never taken the time to reflect fully on the patterns associated with good races, nor had they learned so much from their mental patterns in poor races. Their confidence was enhanced by their having developed an effective plan from studying their own experiences. They knew exactly what they had to do when they arrived at the competition site, at the starting line, and in the race. As the coach put it, "They now have a pattern; they know they are going to do well if they follow the pattern; and they do it."

One of these athletes told me that when she competed against the East German skaters last year, she stood around watching them in awe. However, this year on-site, she and her teammates immediately got busy doing their own preplanned warm-ups and focusing on their own tasks. She had the distinct feeling that "the East Germans were watching us and were wondering why we seemed so confident." And for the first time, these women broke the East German domination of the top spots in speed skating. It was an important psychological breakthrough for them because they then knew that they could come out on top—that it was possible.

To make the race evaluation process most effective, the coach spent 10 to 15 minutes with each of the athletes on the team during the evening after the competition. Together they discussed the race(s). He asked what they felt had gone right, what had gone wrong, and what needed to be improved. He followed the basic questions on the race evaluation form, asking them to verbalize parts of it: For example: What were you thinking here? When you tried this, did it work? What can we do the next time here? The athletes appreciated these individual debriefing sessions and found them particularly helpful when they had not performed well. It helped them pull the important lessons out of the unmet goal and got them back on track. If an athlete felt that an adjustment in the focus plan was needed before the next race or competition, the coach encouraged her to write it into her plan right then and there. On the evening before the subsequent competition, he reminded that athlete to remember what had been discussed and what had to be done.

When an athlete wants to discuss a plan with you, listen to the athlete, draw from what she or he says (*sponge*), and reflect back (*mirror*) her or his best input in an organized way. Then *encourage* specific action from the athlete. To give useful advice for the content of psychological plans, a coach must be a good sponge and a good mirror.

Recognizing Individual Differences

Coach John Bales and Olympic athlete Sue Holloway attended a full-day workshop on attentional styles. They spent the morning filling out self-assessment questionnaires and various forms. From this workshop John learned that he is introverted and likes to withdraw in the face of stress, while Sue is extroverted and likes to mingle. At the competition site, John preferred to withdraw; he had always tried to get Sue to do the same thing, but because of her preference to mingle, she wasn't comfortable with the thought of withdrawing. This insight could have been discovered in a few minutes had John simply asked Sue what she preferred to do before the competition and what she preferred that he do before the competition.

Ask your athletes about preferences, listen closely to the response, and then prepare yourself to act upon that response. What does an athlete want from you as the final word, moments before he or she competes in the arena? As coaches of high-performance athletes, you should know the answer to that question. Sometimes athletes have only one shot to reach their goal in their entire life; it would be helpful if, moments before that one occasion, they could hear something that is likely to do them the most good.

To ensure that there is communication of preferences long before the event, I ask the athletes to write down their responses to the following question: How can the coaching staff best help you this year in competitive situations

- before the event,
- after a good result, and
- after a poor result?

Athletes should be encouraged to clearly communicate preferences. It is better to communicate now, prior to a good result, than to have to do it in retrospect after a poor result. For example, imagine that you are walking with your athlete to the starting line in the finals of the Olympic Games. The next time you will see her or him, the competition will be history. What should you do or say? Does this athlete even want to be walked to the start? Does she or he want to be reminded of anything? It's hard for a coach to be sure of what to say to each athlete or to the team unit without discussing it beforehand.

One thing that has become very clear through my work with high-performance athletes is that they have very different preparation needs. Coaches need to be aware of these individual differences to help athletes achieve their best performances. Treating everyone the same, or expecting everyone to follow the same mental plan, does not work. There are too many individual differences within a team. In some sports, different events or tasks for individual players may require different activation levels or mental plans. You will not get the best from your athletes if you treat them all the same way. Because your athletes are different people with different experiences, you must adapt your approach to meet individual needs. If you don't, you will lose some skilled performances, or you will lose some athletes—in most cases, unnecessarily.

Two highly skilled athletes on our national ski team exemplify the need for an individualized approach from the coach. One of these skiers needs to be challenged; the other needs to be reassured. If the coach approaches these athletes in the same way (particularly before a competition), he will lose one of them—that is almost guaranteed. The first skier likes to be highly activated ("fired up") for her run and performs best when she is in this state. She wants to know that the coach believes in her and wants him to communicate somehow that he has high expectations for her in that race. In our discussions she mentioned, "If the coach gives up on me, then I give up on me." When I asked how she knows he has given up on her, she replied, "when he stops talking to me or gives me the impression, 'don't bother talking to me until you're ready,' I know he has given up." When she perceives the coach as having given up on her or feels as if no one is expecting anything from her, she has the tendency to forget it! She "won't get fired up because it doesn't matter that much." Then everything goes downhill, mentally, because she needs to be fired up to fly.

When she is trying to "psych herself up" for a race, she emphasizes challenge, not reassurance. She performs better in the spotlight. She does well when she feels she must, when she feels she doesn't have a choice, when the challenge is apparent. When she feels that people are counting on her, it helps her get fired up to the appropriate level. Her first World Cup win is a good example of that. It seems that if she's already keen and fired up, she can focus all her energy on doing what she has to do on the way down the hill (hold her race focus). If she's feeling flat, uninspired, or lacking challenge, then during the race most of her energy is expended on trying to keep herself keen and struggling against giving up. Consequently, she is *not focused* on skiing and has difficulty holding her ideal race focus.

The psychological preparation needs of that skier are completely different from those of her equally skilled teammate. If her teammate thinks she *must* do well, she gets caught up in worries that distract from her most productive race focus. The results can be disastrous. She needs to be reassured that she has the ability to perform well but at the same time not made to feel that she *has to* live up to difficult expectations. She needs reassurance more than she needs challenge. She skis best when she is mentally *relaxed*, energized, and focused on her task.

In a situation like this, her coach can help this athlete overcome the little doubts she has about her own abilities and help her believe that she can realize her true potential. To help effectively, the coach should be sure to communicate his complete confidence in her abilities, but not in a way that is likely to raise her level of anxiety or cause worry about meeting his expectations. Quietly, he can calmly reassure her that she is as good as anyone in the world. Perhaps, after good runs, he can point out the quality of her runs and skills by honestly saying, "You are a great skier—you really are!"

Of course these kinds of comments must be based in reality; otherwise, the athlete might think, "He's only saying that." To help this athlete attain a more relaxed race state before a run, perhaps the coach can remind her to call upon her preferred race focus—being relaxed, energized, and centered on the course—because that will allow the unfolding of her technical ability. She needs a quiet display of confidence by the coach, which will imply that she can put it all together.

Positive Feedback

When attempting to help athletes overcome self-doubts, I often relate what their coaches or other coaches have told me about them, things like "She is an incredible athlete; when she is on, no one can touch her—everyone just stands back and watches in awe;" "She is among the best gliders in the world;" "Technically, he is as good as anyone in the world;" "She is the natural athlete . . . unbelievable talent and balance;" "His technique is the best I have ever seen, superior to the world champion." Share these kinds of statements with your athletes if you believe they are accurate assessments of the athletes. On those occasions that I have shared such statements with an athlete, the athlete responded by saying, "The coach has never told me that." As a coach, your reassurance, based on reality, is precisely what many highly skilled athletes need when experiencing some self-doubt.

I have never heard an athlete complain about a coach being too positive. However, I have heard comments like these: "It's good when a coach mentions the *positive* as well as the negative things;" "With a positive comment I think, 'Oh yeah, I can do it!';" "It helps my confidence to hear something positive like 'you can do it';" "I would appreciate more positive feedback from the coach during training;" "At races I would like positive comments from the coaches without any relating to anything negative."

From a motivational perspective and for strengthening self-confidence, positive feedback based on reality is a solid choice. Overemphasis on negative feedback may further damage the athlete's confidence. On several occasions, I have witnessed changes in an athlete's self-confidence as a result of the coaches' communicating complete belief and confidence in that athlete.

You can promote belief and self-confidence in your athletes by being "the first believer." Belief is transmitted by your positiveness, confidence, and patience. Point out progress and good performance. Catch athletes doing things that prove they have the ability to achieve their goal. Your positiveness and projected belief in the athlete hold value even at the highest levels of performance.

Different Approaches

When you are attempting to introduce demanding simulation conditions in training, different approaches are required for various sports and individuals. For example, the Canadian women's field hockey team was preparing for the world championships, which were to be held in the oppressive heat of Malaysia. The coach wanted her athletes to acclimatize by running in 100° heat. Her initial approach was to simply tell her athletes, *do it* (i.e., "don't ask questions. I know what is best for you, just do it!"). This approach will only work with some athletes; others will resist. Another possibility is to allow for more self-direction: You might ask the athletes to think of the goal they have set. Ask them to think of the demands they will face in the championship games and to consider how running in heat will help them prepare for this eventuality. Ask them how important the *goal* is. Is it important enough to justify the extra effort? Leave *them* with the choice (i.e., "it's up to you").

Some athletes do respond better to directives from others. However, most high-performance athletes with whom I have worked respond better to self-direction and the perception of choice. Others prefer a mix of other-direction and self-direction. It helps if coaches know which athletes respond better to either approach. Perhaps you can discover that by talking with your athletes and asking them about their preferences.

Understanding Individual Needs

In order to understand the needs of your athletes, your communication with them has to be two-way; otherwise, nothing is ever really understood or solved. To avoid road blocks, we have to remind ourselves continually of the real purpose of our communication: mutual understanding and mutual benefit. The mutual expression of perspectives is the only route to mutual understanding, and mutual understanding is the first step in meeting athletes' and coaches' needs. The best opportunities for improved mutual understanding come from one-on-one situations without audiences. Most people do not open up in large groups. Many do not even feel comfortable expressing themselves in small groups. Because of this, one-on-one conversations outside the listening range of others provide the best opportunity for mutual exchange, not only between the coach and athlete but for virtually all relationships.

Healthy one-on-one exchanges can occur any place and almost any time. Initially, the least intimidating setting is probably best. Offices, particularly offices that separate people by ownership ("my" office) or by a large executive-type desk or chair, can create artificial barriers. For people who may have difficulty expressing their views, a nonthreatening territory common to both people is initially more conducive to a relaxed mutual exchange. It tends to help break down communication barriers that "authority" sometimes creates. Walking together, running together, having coffee or a soft drink or a bite to eat, sitting in a quiet outdoor setting or after hours in the gym or weightroom—all of these are good situations for developing bonds and resolving conflicts.

Resolving Coach-Athlete Conflicts

When an athlete disagrees with you or expresses a differing perspective, how do you usually respond? Do you try to *win* the verbal exchange or to *understand* the other's perspective? Are you focused on proving you are right and the other person is wrong, or are you focused on trying to understand what that person is saying?

Consider the following scenario:

ATHLETE: When you yelled at me I felt as if you didn't want me here and I felt like not coming back—ever. My motivation was destroyed. (An athlete's *feeling* is being expressed.)

COACH: (Response 1) Yeah, but you deserved it; it's your own fault. You weren't listening; you weren't working. (Here the feeling of the athlete is ignored or rejected. The coach attacks, becomes defensive, and clearly tries to win. Consequently, the athlete feels no acceptance, no resolution is reached, and no solution is shared.)

COACH: (Response 2) I didn't know you were feeling that way [or that strongly]. I feel badly about your being upset. It was not my intent to make you feel that way. What I was trying to do was to [motivate you, keep you on target, etc.] What do you think we can do to resolve this concern? (Here the coach listens, acknowledges the athlete's feelings, expresses her or his response about the athlete's feeling, explains the intent without attacking, and opens the door to seek a solution together. The coach recognizes that by accepting the athlete's feelings, and by sharing both the conversation and solution, he or she can de-escalate the conflict. They are on the same team; they have a common goal.)

Meaningful communication is never a competition. To treat it as such will almost surely prevent any positive outcomes. It is not a game of attack and counterattack. It is a game of understanding. In the communication or harmony game we only win by mutual understanding.

Knowing That You Care

The time that you share with family and team members seems to be the most important index they use to assess caring. Giving time, help, or focus is an action that translates into caring. The absence of such actions is usually interpreted (rightly or wrongly) as not caring.

What makes an athlete or family member feel that you don't care? When you don't pay attention, don't listen, don't talk; when you don't give time, input, or feedback; when you don't seem to want to be with him or her, or when you project a feeling that your focus is someplace else, then you project a lack of caring. When athletes tell me that the coach doesn't care about them, they are usually saying that the coach does not give them enough time, attention, focus, or encouragement.

If a dedicated athlete feels that a coach does not really care, there is a problem that can seriously affect many things: motivation, mood, self-confidence, learning, performance, relationships, satisfaction with sport (and life), and deciding whether to remain with the team. When I have encountered such situations in the coach/ athlete context and have subsequently shared the concern with the coach, it always seems to be received with surprise. I am often left feeling that there is genuine caring on the coach's part, but that the communication or demonstration of the caring has been absent (or at least partially absent).

To show an athlete that you really care

- *give time*—spend time with the person; give the person as much time as possible (compared to other athletes);
- *give help/encouragement*—give assistance, suggestions, feedback, encouragement; do things for the person; and
- *give focus*—be fully *with* the person when with her or him; pay attention to concerns, progress, performance, or changes. Notice changes, and comment constructively on them.

When time together is limited, the expression of caring becomes more important, as does making the best of the limited time together. With limited time, the need is greater for focused time, effective time, or good times. In high-performance amateur sport, your caring is tied closely to perceived commitment. One athlete told me that her performance and motivation would be enhanced by "more coaching support." For her that meant feeling that the coach was totally committed to her and not projecting the idea that she was one of many jobs.

Many dedicated athletes training for the Olympics invest virtually all of themselves in preparation for the Olympic year. They want to see and feel the same commitment from the coach that they see in themselves because that is the way they believe they will get the most out of their own commitment. The only place they can see that is on the water, in the gym, on the field, or in the weight room. They do not *see* all the organizational things that need to be done, even though those things will affect them later if not done. What they clearly see is how much you are with them; they base their judgment of your commitment and caring upon that.

For a head coach (i.e., one responsible for the overall program) who also assumes the responsibility for training certain athletes, perceived commitment can become a problem, especially if he or she cannot always be with the athletes for training sessions. The athletes' perspective seems to be, "If you really cared, if you were really committed to me and to this goal, you would be here with me helping on the water, in the gym, or in the weight room." Of course, caring and commitment can not always be broken down so simply, but the important issue is how a person will interpret your action.

Highly committed athletes cannot clearly comprehend statements about coaches being "too busy" to be with them. It is not unlike children or loved ones who find that time with them is the only, or most clearly comprehensible and tangible, evidence of caring and commitment. Being busy elsewhere is not so clearly understandable because they cannot see it directly, feel it, or *fully* understand it or the priority given to it.

I think it's almost impossible for children to feel that you *really* care unless your *actions* demonstrate it. You have the possibility of alleviating some problems with adults if you are extremely busy or are stretched in various directions by expressing your feelings and caring in other ways. But deep down I guess many of us are still kids. If you do not give people the time they require and you do not express your feelings of caring verbally or physically, they will interpret your actions as meaning you don't care. And that can be devastating. Only action counts—doing something or expressing something. Merely thinking about it does not improve mutual understanding or the perception of caring or commitment.

Communication at the Competition Site

After a recent world championship event, one athlete expressed the feeling that there was very little support or encouragement from the coaches on competition day, either *before* or *after* the event; they seemed to have an aloof attitude. In this case, the coaches probably backed off during the final mental preparation stage because that was how they felt the athletes wanted them to behave. Some athletes wanted this, but others wanted something else. Before the competition begins, you need to know what each athlete expects from you before and after the event.

Coaches can get a good indication of each athlete's preferred pre-event feelings by looking at the Competition Reflections form and by discussing the athlete's impressions of their most recent major competition. For example, when you walked that athlete to the start at the last world championships just before the finals, was he completely satisfied with what you did and said? When you spoke with this athlete just before she stepped on the ice at the World Championships, did she hear what she wanted to hear? For the athlete to feel the best before the event, would he or she prefer that you do or say anything differently this year? Fellow athletes should also become aware of teammates' on-site preferences in order to provide support if possible, or at least to avoid interfering with their on-site preparation, performance, and recovery.

Aside from helping generate the right feelings in preparation for competition, several other situations demand communication and understanding on-site. Specialized plans may need to be altered; or athletes may need help recovering from a loss. As a coach you must be prepared to assist your athletes through such times by utilizing effective communication skills.

Changes in Game Plan

Normally, we like to avoid last-minute changes in routines, programs, play patterns, or game plans. However, occasions arise in which changes become necessary. In such cases, clear communication of the change, followed by mental imagery of the change, can be very useful.

If there is a possible condition change or potential problem spot, the coach should encourage the athlete(s) to focus attention on what to *do* to correct the problem, rather than focusing attention on what *not* to do. Once the athlete clearly understands what is being asked, he or she can try to imagine (i.e., see or feel oneself) going through the new movement pattern successfully several times before actually stepping onto the floor, court, field, or course.

It is important to phrase instructions positively in a variety of coaching situations. Changing strategies or plans is one of them. It is better to begin a statement with a do than with a don't. Let me demonstrate why. I'm going to ask you *not* to do a few things.

- Don't think of an orange.
- Don't think of an egg.
- Don't think of your favorite drink.

How did you do? What image came into your mind? Chances are that you created an image of those things I asked you not to think about. Athletes do the same thing. For that reason, when giving feedback to athletes, state what you want them to *do* in positive, concrete terms. For example, say "Remember to focus on....," rather than "Don't do that"; ask athletes to think of "calm and relaxed" instead of telling them "don't be anxious."

In a sport like alpine skiing, sometimes last-minute instructions based on changing course conditions are relayed back up the hill to an athlete. From my experience often when a skier was told that there was a problem at a specific point on the hill, the skier went off the hill precisely at that point. "Sometimes when feedback comes up, it can stick in your mind." "Maybe telling me it was hard made it harder than it was." "I went off... coach said I froze." One athlete recalled an occasion in which, after pointing out a trouble spot, the coach said, "For God's sake, this time don't screw up." Sure enough, she went off at that point.

Most of our skiers valued the information coming back up the hill but felt it could be more valuable and much more useful if it were relayed more constructively. Telling an athlete what not to do does not seem to help matters. If, however, the coach can calmly tell an athlete specifically what to do rather than what not to do, that is helpful. It allows the athlete to run that constructive sequence, "doing it" in mental imagery, and go—most often without an overload of worry or a lingering thought about *not* doing something.

When I spoke with the coach about a remedy for this concern, he first confirmed the accuracy of the athletes' comments about his feedback. He indicated a probable reason for it. During the heat of the competition, he is usually excited, especially if a skier has just gone off the course at 70 miles an hour. He wants to transmit the information about the trouble spot quickly and usually just blurts out something. Only after he starts or finishes relaying the message does he realize that it wasn't very effective. By then it is too late.

In this situation, clearly the medium is a big part of the message. The manner of transmitting the message is being carefully read. Speed of talk, tone of voice, and projection of excitation or worry are all important. If the information itself is transmitted in a negative fashion, that complicates the problem even more.

The strategy we discussed, which he subsequently used successfully, was to write out a cue word ("reflect"—don't react) on a piece of tape and stick it to the walkie-talkie that he used for transmitting messages up the hill. At the competition site, before speaking, he always looked at the walkie-talkie. Seeing "reflect" signaled the following action: a deep breath (pause); a momentary reflection about what the athlete should *do* to avoid the problem; then, in a calm, collected, and confident voice, a message relayed in a positive way. If the message happened to begin in an excited, worried, or negative way...he would *stop* and say, "Hold it. I'll start over again.'' Then he did so, relaying the message in the way that was likely to do the most good. In this case, because the athletes knew the coach was attempting to improve the positiveness of his feedback, they understood and approved of redirection, even in midstream.

At the end of the season, I asked the coach how this strategy had worked, and he said, ''I think I improved. At least I was able to catch myself a lot more. Once you have awareness, you have anything half beat.''

Communication After Loss

Some athletes have told me that their coaches do not relate well to them or to other athletes when they are not performing well. How good are you at communicating with athletes who have just experienced an important loss or have failed to achieve an important goal? I have noticed that after a loss, there is often no communication with the athlete; he is left alone with his loss. In such circumstances, how does the athlete interpret the lack of communication? Is it perceived as supportive or nonsupportive, caring or uncaring? Communication with people who are faced with a loss is often difficult because we feel uncomfortable and don't know what to say or do. This is true not only for a loss in sport but also for the loss of loved ones through sickness, separation, or death. Sometimes it is useful for us to express our feelings of uncertainty about how we should best respond or help.

What most people want and need when trying to cope with a loss is *support*. ''I care about you, I love you, I'm here if you need anything''—that is what needs to be communicated. Sometimes it can be said through physical contact; sometimes it can be felt with a few simple words of support. After loss in sport, ignoring is seldom the most constructive pattern to follow, for it can be interpreted as a form of rejection or as if you do not care. Negative criticism or fingerpointing is even worse because it tends to unnecessarily degrade someone who is already down. It is better to go to the people, share their disappointment, and listen to their thoughts and feelings about what happened out there. If you go to the people and they prefer to be alone, they can tell you, ''Not now, Coach." If you do not go to them and they do want your support, it is difficult for them to tell you.

Generally we should offer support first and look for the lessons in the loss at another time. In some ways it is like meeting the immediate needs of a child who gets hurt. The child wants to be held and comforted (physically and psychologically) *before* hearing you say what should or should not have been done. If you jump to the lesson too quickly, it will be lost.

If you think about how you might best respond to loss (or victory) in sport and discuss it with the athletes before it occurs, you will have a much better idea of how each athlete prefers that you respond. Advance communication of preferred responses probably gives you the best chance of being positive and growth-oriented. During a discussion of preferences between a group of athletes and their coach, one of the athletes commented that in important loss situations she acts as if she wants to be alone but really wants "someone to come over and put an arm around me. I want a hug." Another athlete said that initially he wants to be alone and then wants support and discussion. Each athlete is different. You must make the effort to understand those differences and respond to them effectively.

In terms of meeting athletes needs after a loss, we have found it particularly helpful for the coach to make use of the Postcompetition Evaluation form. By going through the evaluation form with the athlete, the coach can constructively and objectively point out good and not-so-good points and can then help the athlete focus on ways to improve performance for the next event or competition.

Sometimes it takes something dramatic to force us to think about our own patterns. The following is one such case. A few days after a poor performance at a "critical" competition, a talented young athlete took her own life. She had high performance expectations for herself and, perhaps more important in this context, felt heavy demands placed upon her by loved ones.

I did not know her personally but knew others who were at the competition who knew her well. I asked how she responded immediately after her loss. Apparently there were no immediate signs of overreaction; in fact, I was told that outwardly she showed no emotional reaction at all, which for her was strange. I asked whether, after her performance, anyone went over to her at the competition site to be with her, to offer support, to listen, to talk. No one had. She was left to herself, with her own thoughts.

I realize that hindsight will never be of any value to this athlete or to her family. However, I cannot help but feel that if she had been helped to recognize her own value *outside sport* and had thought about it before this event, she would be alive today. That is one of the reasons I include the goal of self-acceptance on the Goals form that you distributed at the first mental training meeting of the season (i.e., Can you make a commitment to accept yourself and learn from the experience, regardless of whether you achieve your ultimate performance goal this year?).

I also feel that if she had been given some solid support after the event and had the opportunity to express some of her inner feelings, she might have been able to keep things in perspective. That is one of the reasons I encourage coaches and others to go to the athletes and lend support after losses. They need to know that you care about them as people and that you are there if they need you.

Frequently when people behave in a manner that is "out-of-character," it signals trouble. In situations like that, communication is especially important. When an athlete who normally expresses emotion after loss becomes withdrawn and emotionless, it is "out-of-character." You should immediately communicate with that athlete even if the initial communication is limited to a simple display of support or a suggestion of getting together to talk later.

By offering your support you can clearly demonstrate that you are capable of separating a person from his or her performance, and that a person's essence and importance extends beyond any performance. You can love and accept the person even though you are not in love with the performance.

CHAPTER 8

Planning for Major Competitions

You may or may not have the opportunity to sit down and share ideas with a group of experienced Olympic coaches before a major competition like the Olympics or world championships. But you do have the opportunity to sit down with your own team before every major competition to discuss specific distractors that are likely to occur and ways to avoid or cope with them. This is particularly useful for less seasoned athletes. Wherever possible, draw upon the knowledge of people who have already been there: veteran members of the team, former athletes or coaches, or other people who have "lived" in that environment. They can help familiarize athletes with possible distractors and tell them what to expect as well as suggest strategies for minimizing those distractions.

When going through this familiarization process, team members can be divided into small groups and asked to list as many distractors and solution routes as possible. They should fully explore the potential problem area they are addressing, without rushing. Solutions should be oriented toward the best interest of the athletes' performances.

Knowing what to expect and what is "normal" under these less-than-ideal conditions can be a big help. Transportation delays, customs procedures, waiting for baggage, accreditation, femininity tests, picking up uniforms that don't fit, drug tests, food, accommodations, security, telegrams, telephone calls, well-wishers, autograph seekers, media, and other distractions can be extremely unnerving if you and your team are not prepared for them.

Clearing the Path for Performance

Sport administrators, officials, managers, organizers, and committee members sometimes inadvertently create barriers and additional obstacles for athletes. The job of the coach and team officials is to reduce hassles as much as possible, particularly those that are unrelated to performing at the actual event. The job of the athlete is to prepare him- or herself to perform and to be prepared to avoid or face any hassles that might arise.

Larry Cain, 1984 Olympic champion in canoeing, made some interesting comments at our final training camp directly before the Olympics, comments that relate to how coaches and leaders can help clear the path for excellence. As the event approached, Larry felt a need or strong desire to be more in control of daily choices that affected his life. He did not want to be overorganized by others, to be rushed, or to be told that he had to do this or that (especially off the water). His advice and plea was to "keep it low key," to be "flexible," and to "let people do stuff their own way as much as possible." In the final days before and during the Games, he felt that being allowed his "own space was more important than ever." He wanted to start withdrawing from the group in order to begin his own mental preparation for his event. Inflexibility with respect to understanding individual needs or ordering people around in a seemingly insensitive way "can ruin a good feeling," a good feeling that coaches and athletes have been working all year to create.

Sylvie Bernier, 1984 Olympic 3-meter diving champion, made a similar point when she emphasized the importance of an athlete "getting what she wants" before an important competition: for example, time alone, training times, meals, and accommodation. Coaches and team leaders should do everything possible to meet athletes' needs and preferences prior to events like the Olympic Games because that can affect the athletes' mental state, which in turn will influence performance.

To free Sylvie to perform at the Olympic Games, Elizabeth Jack, 1984 Olympic diving coach/manager for the Canadian team, outlined the most important facets of her coaching role at the Olympic site.

- Provide *zero* (or minimal) technical input or suggestions for technical changes.
- Remain calm and confident throughout—a worried coach results in a worried athlete.
- Handle disorganization—travel, training, living quarters.
- Relieve added pressures—media, home court advantage, feelings of enclosure.

In order to help create the ideal mental state for athletic excellence, consider doing whatever you can to insulate the athlete from as many environmental obstacles and additional demands as possible. The prime areas of concern include hassles relating to travel, delays, uniforms, equipment, food, money, briefings, and red tape. Whatever essential tasks or information that can be given to the athlete before arrival at the Games should be addressed before arrival to lessen the "overload factor." Free the athletes to do what they came to do. They already have to cope with many demands quite apart from the event, so don't add to them. Of course, in reality the athletes will face obstacles at important competitions. Help them anticipate and prepare for the "outside" demands so they are able to cope with them constructively.

Keeping Training Camps Positive

Some coaches and athletes have expressed a concern about the psychological effects of extended training camps leading up to the Olympics. When living in close quarters with not much to do but train, compete, and think about the upcoming event, people can become tense, restless, bored, and short-tempered and may begin to "get on each other's nerves." I asked our summer Olympic coaches if they had any thoughts on how to keep boredom and interpersonal conflicts to a minimum. What follows is an outline of their responses.

Plan Social and Leisure Activities

- Have planned breaks, interesting entertainment, organized and unorganized social activities, short sightseeing trips, and recreational activities.
- Suggest that the athletes bring things with which they can entertain themselves: for example, a guitar, harmonica, audio and video cassette tapes, cards, cribbage board, table games, books, chess set, camera, frisbee, football, baseball, bingo, jacks, swimming gear, interesting hobbies, paints & brushes, or things to create. They can write poems, letters, articles, songs, jokes, or books; and/or they can draw, sketch, carve, or paint.
- Encourage them to maintain communication with home and home life through letters and phone calls or establish interpersonal contacts outside the camp.
- Have short clinics or workshops on anything of possible interest to athletes.
- Help make sure athletes have something interesting to do.

Plan for Variety

- Plan greater variety in the training program.
- Vary the location of camp.
- Vary the camp composition by rotating training partners, by dividing large groups into small groups, by having separate camps for separate factions of the team, by having camps for the whole national team and camps that mix national team members with athletes from other countries.

Plan for Roommates

- Select roommates carefully.
- Possibly rotate roommates now and then.
- Attempt to accommodate for individual preference for roommates and for training partners.

Plan Time Off

- Schedule days off. Have 3 days training to 1 day off, and a 3 to 5 day break so that athletes and coaches can go off and do other things.
- Publicize the schedule indicating time off.

Plan for Open Communication

- Try to anticipate problems and head them off early by seeking athlete input.
- Discuss problems openly; face the issues.
- Allow for open dialogue and discussion sessions not aimed at a personal level but at a team harmony level.
- Open the communication channels between coaches and athletes.
- Create a family atmosphere.
- Cultivate tolerance and patience.
- Create an atmosphere of mutual love and respect for teammates.
- Above all, keep the communication positive.

Simulate "Normal" Conditions

- Duplicate a normal lifestyle as much as possible, except at specific camps that are designed to simulate the competition environment.
- Allow athletes and coaches the option of bringing spouses and children with them to some camps.

Shorten Camps

- Leave athletes and coaches in a "normal" home situation as long as possible.
- Think about whether extended camps are the best preparation route for an Olympic effort, particularly in individual sports.
- Keep training camps to a minimum; shorten their duration.

Other Suggestions (For Overcoming Problems with Extended Camps)

- Supply good food that attempts to accommodate for individual preferences in menu.
- Provide good accommodations.
- Select positive coaches who keep the focus constructive. One coach responded that "a bored athlete is a direct result of a bored coach, and the problem should be approached from that angle."
- Try to maintain a relaxed atmosphere.
- Set social harmony goals.

- Above all, remind your athletes of the goals and objectives they have set.

Final Camp Before the Olympics

Our final three-week training camp for the Olympic Canoe Team was held in California just before the 1984 Games. It was one of the most positive camps I have experienced. Some factors not directly related to the training facility that helped were

- single rooms for all athletes and coaches;
- good food with choice of menu;
- buffet style service (no waiting around to be served);
- movies twice a day (chosen by the athletes and shown on the video) to fill the lulls between the early morning and early evening training sessions, shown in a common team lounge area;
- enough vehicles (5) so that people could get to and from the training site easily, flexibly, and without delay; and
- a location that allowed easy access to the city and to nearby resort areas for days or time off.

CHAPTER 9

Year-End
Evaluation

At the end of the season, you should get together as a team if possible. A final meeting is a good opportunity to wrap things up on a positive note, to point out some good things that happened during the year, some goals that were met, and some goals that can still be met. It is also a good time to get some constructive feedback on the year's program, especially on the psychological training component.

I have included a general year-end evaluation form that was originally developed by Olympic Ski Coach Currie Chapman and later adapted by Frank Garner, Olympic Canoe Coach. Both coaches found it an effective tool for obtaining useful information from their athletes. I have also included a year-end evaluation form specifically designed to assess your mental training program. If possible, distribute these evaluation forms to team members at a final team meeting; otherwise, distribute them through the mail.

General Year-End Evaluation Form

The General Year-End Evaluation form found on pages 75-78 can be distributed as is for most sports. In some cases minor adaptations may be required. The form will clarify the athletes' perspective on the strengths and weaknesses of your overall program as well as provide specific suggestions on ways of better meeting their needs.

Year-End Evaluation of Mental Training Program

In addition to a General Year-End Evaluation, it is useful to conduct a specific evaluation of the mental training program, especially after the first year or two of its operation. The Year-End Evaluation form on pages 80-84 was designed to assess athletes' and coaches' perceptions of the effects of various components in the mental training program. Before distributing the form to your athletes and coaches, make sure all major components of your mental training program are listed in the left-hand column of the form under the heading Program Components.

Year-End Evaluation of Sport Psychology Consultant

If you use a sport psychology consultant as part of your program, it is a good idea to have the athletes and coaches evaluate his or her effectiveness. The evaluation form that is provided on pages 85-87 was developed in conjunction with John Partington and can be distributed as it stands in almost all cases. It will give a clear picture of the strengths and weaknesses of the consultant and suggest ways that he or she can better meet the athlete's needs.

General Year-End Evaluation

In order to evaluate and improve our program we must have the athlete's opinion about *what* was done and *how* it was done. Indicate by the words *excellent, good, average, fair,* and *poor* how you evaluate the different aspects of the program this past season.

I. *General Evaluation*
    1. *Team Program:* (through season)
        Organization _____
        Enthusiasm of staff _____
        Moral support of staff _____
        Technical expertise of staff _____
        Off-event program _____
        On-event training _____
        Team performance _____
        Team morale _____
        Comments:

        _____
        _____
        _____
        _____
        _____

    2. *Personal Program:* (through season)
        Your organization _____
        Your mental attitude _____
        Your physical condition _____
        Your technical execution _____
        Your commitment to winning _____
        Your tolerance of people, events, situations _____
        Comments:

        _____
        _____
        _____
        _____
        _____

    3. Identify one aspect of the past season's program that you want to see repeated next season.

        _____
        _____
        _____
        _____
        _____
        _____

(Cont.)

General Year-End Evaluation (Cont.)

    4. Identify one aspect of the past season's program that you want to see avoided/deleted next season.

         _____

         _____

         _____

    5. List those aspects of the program that should be improved/reviewed by the staff for the upcoming season.

         _____

         _____

         _____

         _____

         _____

    6. Briefly comment on personal strengths and areas needing improvement for each member of the support staff.

         _____

         _____

         _____

         _____

         _____

    7. Analyze your performance in the past season and indicate what you need to do to improve.

         _____

         _____

         _____

         _____

         _____

         _____

         _____

II. *Scheduling and Emphasis:*
Please comment on the following areas of the past year's program and competitive season.

    1. Rest and time off: _____

         _____

(Cont.)

General Year-End Evaluation (Cont.)

   2. Training sites: _____

       _____

       _____

       _____

       _____

   3. Length of training camps: _____

       _____

       _____

   4. Amount of technique work: _____

       _____

       _____

       _____

   5. Number of competitions: _____

       _____

       _____

   6. Number of athletes involved: _____

       _____

       _____

   7. Availability of support staff: _____

       _____

       _____

III. *General Preparation Macrocycle*

   1. Are you satisfied with your off-season program? If not, why?

       _____

   2. Any suggestions to improve our general preparation?

       _____

       _____

       _____

       _____

(Cont.)

General Year-End Evaluation (Cont.)

IV. *Next Year's Program*

    1. Do you feel we need to do anything special to the program to "peak" for the championships (e.g., Worlds or Olympics)?

    _____

    _____

    _____

    _____

    _____

    2. What do you feel you can realistically achieve this upcoming season?

    World ranking: _____

    Olympic results: _____

    Other achievements: _____

    _____

    _____

    3. What are your long-term goals in this sport (after this season)?

    _____

    _____

    _____

    _____

    4. What do you see as your strengths, your weaknesses, and specific areas to improve upon?

    Weaknesses: _____

    _____

    _____

    Strengths: _____

    _____

    _____

    Specific areas to improve: _____

    _____

    _____

    _____

    _____

By carefully examining the responses to each of the Year-End Evaluation forms, you will be one step closer to refining the preparation of your athletes. Take the time to learn from these evaluations just as your athletes have learned from their ongoing performance evaluations.

Year-End Evaluation of Mental Training Program

The purpose of this evaluation is to determine to what extent (if any) you feel the mental training program to which you were exposed affected you. Please use the scale below (in which −5 indicates "hindered," 0 indicates "no effect," and 5 indicates "helped a lot") to express how you feel each of the Program Components listed below affected you with respect to pursuing your personal goals this year.

I. Program Component	Hindered, Interfered	No effect Didn't help Didn't hurt	Helped a lot	Program Component Not Done (ND)
Team meeting(s) on mental preparation	−5 −4 −3 −2 −1	0	1 2 3 4 5	ND
Individual meetings(s) on psych plans with coach	−5 −4 −3 −2 −1	0	1 2 3 4 5	ND
Individual meeting(s) on psych plans with sport psychology consultant	−5 −4 −3 −2 −1	0	1 2 3 4 5	ND
Readings on psych preparation in *Psyching for Sport*	−5 −4 −3 −2 −1	0	1 2 3 4 5	ND
Setting specific goals	−5 −4 −3 −2 −1	0	1 2 3 4 5	ND
Precompetition plan	−5 −4 −3 −2 −1	0	1 2 3 4 5	ND
Competition focus plan	−5 −4 −3 −2 −1	0	1 2 3 4 5	ND

Refocusing plan	−5 −4 −3 −2 −1	0	1 2 3 4 5	ND
Competition simulation	−5 −4 −3 −2 −1	0	1 2 3 4 5	ND
Practice of focusing during training	−5 −4 −3 −2 −1	0	1 2 3 4 5	ND
Mental imagery	−5 −4 −3 −2 −1	0	1 2 3 4 5	ND
Relaxation	−5 −4 −3 −2 −1	0	1 2 3 4 5	ND
Postcompetition evaluation forms	−5 −4 −3 −2 −1	0	1 2 3 4 5	ND
Team meeting(s) on team harmony	−5 −4 −3 −2 −1	0	1 2 3 4 5	ND
Interpersonal communication plan	−5 −4 −3 −2 −1	0	1 2 3 4 5	ND
Media plan	−5 −4 −3 −2 −1	0	1 2 3 4 5	ND
Overall mental training program	−5 −4 −3 −2 −1	0	1 2 3 4 5	ND
Other areas (fill in)	−5 −4 −3 −2 −1	0	1 2 3 4 5	ND

II. Over the course of the season,

	Less aware	Same, no change	Much more aware
Did you become any more or less aware of the kind of preevent thinking that contributes to your best performance(s)?	-5 -4 -3 -2 -1	0	1 2 3 4 5
Did you become any more or less aware of the kind of focus within the event that contributes to your best performance(s)?	-5 -4 -3 -2 -1	0	1 2 3 4 5

III. Over the course of the season, did you experience any changes in your ability to:

	Got worse	Same	Much improved
Constructively refocus before the event (when needed)?	-5 -4 -3 -2 -1	0	1 2 3 4 5
Constructively refocus within the event (when needed)?	-5 -4 -3 -2 -1	0	1 2 3 4 5
Get the most out of *each* training session?	-5 -4 -3 -2 -1	0	1 2 3 4 5
Draw constructive lessons from setbacks or errors?	-5 -4 -3 -2 -1	0	1 2 3 4 5
Communicate openly or effectively?	-5 -4 -3 -2 -1	0	1 2 3 4 5

IV. How much do you feel the overall Mental Training Program affected:	Hindered	No effect	Helped a lot
a. The positiveness of your thinking?	-5 -4 -3 -2 -1	0	1 2 3 4 5
b. Your feelings of personal control?	-5 -4 -3 -2 -1	0	1 2 3 4 5
c. The consistency of your performance?	-5 -4 -3 -2 -1	0	1 2 3 4 5

V. Where do you think you need the most work to continue to improve and refine your psychological skills?

VI. Do you have any suggestions that you would like to see included as part of next season's Mental Training Program?

VII. Any other comments concerning this evaluation form or the Mental Training Program?

Year-End Evaluation of Sport Psychology Consultant

Based on your personal feelings, please assess the sport psychology consultant who worked with the team this past year.

1. What were his or her strengths?

2. What were his or her weaknesses?

3. In what way (if any) did he or she help you?

4. In what ways could he or she help you more, or better meet your needs?

(Cont.)

Year-End Evaluation of Sport Psychology Consultant (Cont.)

5. Rate his or her overall effect:

	Hindered, interfered					No effect	Helped a lot				
Effect on you	−5	−4	−3	−2	−1	0	1	2	3	4	5
Effect on team	−5	−4	−3	−2	−1	0	1	2	3	4	5
Effect on coach	−5	−4	−3	−2	−1	0	1	2	3	4	5

6. Rate his or her characteristics:

Consultant Characteristics	Not at all										Yes, definitely
Had *useful knowledge* about mental training that seemed to apply directly to me.	0	1	2	3	4	5	6	7	8	9	10
Seemed willing to provide an *individualized mental training program* based on *my input and needs*.	0	1	2	3	4	5	6	7	8	9	10
Seemed open, flexible and *ready to collaborate/cooperate* with me.	0	1	2	3	4	5	6	7	8	9	10
Had a *positive, constructive attitude.*	0	1	2	3	4	5	6	7	8	9	10
Proved to be *trustworthy*.	0	1	2	3	4	5	6	7	8	9	10
Was *easy for me to relate to* (e.g., I felt comfortable and understood).	0	1	2	3	4	5	6	7	8	9	10
Fitted in with others connected with the team.	0	1	2	3	4	5	6	7	8	9	10
Tried to *help me draw upon my strengths* (i.e., the things that already worked for me) in order to make my best performance more consistent.	0	1	2	3	4	5	6	7	8	9	10

(Cont.)

Year-End Evaluation of Sport Psychology Consultant (Cont.)

Consultant Characteristics	Not at all									Yes, definitely

Tried to *help me overcome possible problems*, or weaknesses, in order to make my best performance event better and more consistent.

0 1 2 3 4 5 6 7 8 9 10

Provided clear, practical, concrete strategies for me to try out in an attempt to solve problems or improve the level and consistency of my performance.

0 1 2 3 4 5 6 7 8 9 10

7. For next year, what would you recommend?

- Retain her or his services. _____

- Retain her or his services with some changes. _____
  (list changes here:)

- Replace her or him with someone else. _____

- Do not retain and do not replace. _____

8. Any other comments?

Making Things Happen

My mental training program was designed to help athletes prepare themselves to deal with the variety of psychological concerns that Olympic coaches and athletes had raised. I initially introduced and refined this program with several national teams over a period of 3 years. I then asked two coaches, Bob Northrop, a U.S. swim coach, and Lorraine Laframboise, a Canadian equestrian coach, if they would like to try introducing it to their athletes on their own. Both were receptive to doing so.

Northrop and Laframboise were given the same basic information that you have in this book: a detailed guide outlining what to do at each mental training meeting and some detailed information for the athletes to read, drawn from *Psyching for Sport: Mental Training for Athletes*. At the conclusion of their first experience with this mental training program, they provided me with some feedback.

What You Can Expect

To give you some idea of what you can expect to get out of the program, I decided to share their comments with you now, before you implement your own program.

BOB NORTHROP: I would like to share some of my thoughts after completing this initial attempt at mental training with my team.

The structure of the program answered a long-time need for me. Since beginning to coach, I had nagging feelings and strong beliefs about the importance of the mind in all endeavors—not just sport. Unfortunately, my own insecurity led me to do what most of us do: stay with the familiar, the tried and true methods of training. The emphasis was on physical training. All the books told you how—that is what coaches talked about, that is what athletes knew—it was comfortable, it was easy. This program required some thought to adapt it to our situation, but the structure was based on ideas that reinforced my intuitive feelings. The specific topics and forms gave me a means, a method, to try. They also gave me the confidence to try. I had wanted to do more, particularly with the mental side, but lacked the tools. Here are the tools.

At first I was nervous. This was new ground and I was shaky. I knew I wanted to do it but was unsure of how the athletes would receive it. I perspired a lot in those first meetings, especially when my initial remarks were greeted with silence.

However, by the third meeting I settled down. They were getting involved, asking questions of me and of each other, and volunteering their experiences and ideas relating to the topics. In the end, it was fun. I enjoyed the give and take, and they seemed to enjoy talking about how they felt and how to get better prepared to meet various situations.

Once I began talking about various aspects of mental training at the meetings, I knew that the concepts were right, and I wanted to expand them into other areas of sport and life. My confidence increased. I found that it was easy to translate the ideas of the meetings into action in practice and in competitive situations. My manner "on-the-deck" became more expressive, and I often reminded athletes of ideas discussed in the meetings. I liked my reaction very much and believed that I coached better. We didn't become "friends," but we did become "comrades" working toward commonly understood goals with mutually agreed-upon assumptions.

I used to be afraid to treat individuals differently for fear of offending some. But this way, the uniqueness of each individual becomes clear, and everyone seems to understand the concept of individuality as each separate part brings its contribution to the whole. Each individual part must be complete in order to make the endeavor the best it can be. It changes the mechanical way of looking at sport and infuses an exciting variety of colors—for each individual. I liked doing it, and I think that the athletes enjoyed it, also. They seemed to take with them specific, concrete ideas. They reported using cues often. They now plan races, whereas they never took the time before. They tried to become aware of their self-talk and worked at positive, emotional self-statements. Those who used the prerace warm-up strategy with vigorous physical activity immediately before the race reported great success. The general response was positive with many "I can't wait until next year" comments. I can't either. I enjoyed it and am anxious to expand on the basic structure next time.

LORRAINE LAFRAMBOISE: At first I felt quite unqualified because I had no formal background in psychology. I was still very green with the devices and structure of such a system. I remember walking into the first meeting feeling anxious. The athletes were cracking jokes and digging into corn chips as if they hadn't been fed in a week. I said to myself, "OK. . . calm . . you did feel that this was a good idea—didn't you? Otherwise why would you have set this up? Right. OK." A few restless moments passed as I hovered on the edge. Then I began, and the worries I had feared never came to pass.

During that first goal-setting meeting with my athletes, I realized that together we were touching on life plans, and the relevance of my position became apparent. That first year I found myself traveling along a logical and practical path that seemed to be taking us in the right general direction, but I really didn't know where we'd end up.

It wasn't long before I could see definite and, in some cases, dramatic improvements in concentration and consistency in performance. By the second year, my own confidence in the basic system was up and things were really cooking. That year one of my young up-and-coming riders placed first among the Canadians in all three Olympic trials.

I feel quite strongly that in the past 2 years, I owe 70% to 90% of the steady successes of my athletes to our mental training program. The last 10% to 30%? Well, my athletes' ability and my talent, of course!

Here are some of the major points that helped me:

* *Time was redefined for me*—time for the coach to listen, time for the athlete to speak, time for both to think. It became obvious that the time set aside to quietly savor victory or to study defeat also allowed an unrestricted opportunity for the athlete to com-

municate with the coach and more importantly, with him- or herself.

- *Mental imagery and positive self-talk* were two of the most important devices in the mental training program, especially for dealing with distractions that required refocusing.
- *Daily application and practice* of the basic techniques in training and warm-up were necessary for success.
- *Behavior patterns that emerged during the stress of competition* could be isolated and identified through the program. It therefore became easy for coach and athlete to gain insight into coping with or avoiding performance-deterring tendencies.

The successful athlete must learn to deal readily with the distractions and unplanned interferences that necessitate refocusing. These arise at every competition, as well as at many training sessions, and are the cause of most if not all disappointing performances. With a mental training program, things don't go wrong; they *happen* and become tools to make things go even better than before. The real virtue of this mental training program is that the self-learning process is maximized.

I was rather unprepared for one thing that did happen as this program progressed. Both my athletes and I came to know ourselves more than we had anticipated. Athletes began to understand themselves and the subtleties of their performances better. This gave them the ability to teach themselves. They became more self-directed, and their need for my "holding their hand" decreased substantially. This left me freer to coach technically and tactically and left athletes with more time to concentrate on achieving their goals.

In the future, if I hear a fellow coach protest that he doesn't have the time or energy to introduce a mental training program, I will quietly take him aside and extol the virtues of such a program—or smile and walk away, knowing I'm one up on him.

Focusing Skills

In high-level sport *performance*, mental activities are rarely separated from physical activities. Consequently, when training mental skills, it is often best to practice them in combination with physical skills. The advantage of an on-site approach to mental training is that it is "real": it has real applicability, it is done in the real situation, and it is more acceptable to athletes. Therefore, the mental skills are more likely to get done and practiced.

The following are some examples of on-site practice that combine mental and physical activity:

- Scanning the body and relaxing tense areas at specific times while engaged in the activity
- "Imaging" a skill or race strategy just before physically performing it within the training session
- Practicing cue words or self-talk to refocus attention in the face of distraction caused by the coach, by the game, by other athletes, or by physical cues such as tiredness from the body
- Having athletes visualize one thing they would like to accomplish in today's training session and then encouraging them to "let it happen" during the training session as it did in imagery
- Having athletes focus on relaxation between certain training intervals and on energizing thoughts during tired times in practice
- Focusing on different cue words related to power, flow, or technique that can initially be called out by the coach at specific times during the activity.

To help runners practice focusing *while running*, track coach Andy Higgins (1979) devised the following cues:

- **Think "tall"**—this means *erect*, with *full extension* of the legs. The opposite is "sitting down" when running.

- **Think "relaxed"**—this means *move easily*, as opposed to tensing and "working hard" to move. Let the movements of running *flow*. Keep the *shoulders low* and the arms swinging *rhythmically* by the sides.

- **Think "smoothly"**—this means *float* across the top of the ground. All motion should be *forward*, not up and down. Leg action should be *efficient* and *rhythmic*. The legs should move easily under the body like a wheel rolling smoothly along.

Once the essence of these cues has been discussed with the athletes, the coach can call out the cues one at a time while the athletes are running (e.g., "tall," "relax," "smooth"). Similar kinds of focus cues can be applied to a variety of other skills and sports.

Simulating Stress

When preparing athletes to face stressful conditions by simulating the stressful event, it is important to provide appropriate strategies for channeling the stress *before* introducing the stress. Otherwise the stressful condition will likely result in a poor performance and stress-related problems. It is of no value to load on stress without first loading on strategies to deal with it. If you plan to increase demands in training or lead-up competitions, make sure, first, that the athletes know why you are doing it, and second, that they have a plan for effectively dealing with the increase. Frequently, the best strategy to effectively deal with increased stress is to encourage athletes to concentrate fully on their competition focus plan.

Coaches Mental State

You should consider working on your own psychological skills, your own plan for coping with stress, and your own communication plan, especially for high-stress conditions. You face different demands in competitive situations just as your athletes do. When you experience more stress you are also more likely to react without first considering the consequences.

The coaching skills that are most appropriate at a competition site may be quite different from those that are most useful during training. In training, not only is the coach more relaxed but he or she may spend much of his or her time trying to teach, to correct, and to motivate. In competitive situations, these roles may no longer be useful. It is too late to teach skills, and most athletes are already "up" for the event. The most important coaching skills at the high-level competition site may be maintaining or projecting a calm confident perspective in the face of stress or providing support.

If you are serious about becoming a better on-site coach, you can complete the Competition Reflections form provided in chapter 3, using your own best and worst coaching performances as referents. You can also ask athletes how they would prefer that you behave on-site. Once you have done this, draw upon those experiences to develop your own preevent plan, competition focus plan, and refocusing plan to enable you to perform your best. Then work on refining those plans through ongoing self-evaluations.

Endings and Beginnings

I hope that the end of this book is the beginning of your action with respect to introducing a mental training program. I invite you to act in the following ways:

- Start a mental training program this year. Begin by holding your first mental training meeting. The rest will follow from there.
- Help athletes develop a greater awareness of how the content, intensity, and direction of their self-talk affects their feelings, focus, and performance in training and competitions.
- Encourage each athlete to look at her or his personal history of successes for the kind of awareness, focus, and self-talk that was most effective in previous best performances. Then, suggest they try refining that approach and making it more consistent.
- Help athletes develop a specific precompetition plan that includes both physical and mental activity, especially for the last 15 minutes before the start. The mental activity may include a mental review of the game plan, positive reminders of overall readiness and best-event focus, and cues to relax or activate, depending upon individual needs.
- Encourage athletes to develop an effective event focus plan.
- Encourage athletes to develop a refocusing plan that can be used before, during, or after the event.
- Expect individual differences, and work to fulfill each person's specific needs; the precise situation and mental strategy for improvement may be different for each individual.
- Find out what your athletes prefer at the competition site. How does each athlete prefer that you behave before the event, between events, and after good and bad performances? Become practiced at doing what will assist each athlete on-site.
- Ensure that athletes competing together on the same unit are aware of each other's preferences regarding on-site psycholog-

ical preparation. This will help ensure that they do not interfere with each other's preparation for a maximum performance.
- Practice doing what will help you cope and function well under high-stress conditions. Think about your own preferences.
- Ensure that opportunities are set up for athletes and coaches to practice precompetitive and competitive strategies such as preplanned self-talk, cue words, focusing, and refocusing techniques in time-trials and in simulated competitions. When preparing for very important events, if possible, simulate the competition day from beginning to end.
- Devise opportunities for practicing relevant focusing skills that can be included as part of training sessions, and encourage athletes to use them.
- Develop an action plan for improved team harmony and interpersonal communication.
- *Smile.* You are on the right path.

As this book draws to an end, I have the feeling that I have become part of a relay team. I have run the first leg and placed the baton in your hand. You must run the second leg and place the baton in the hands of your athletes. We are all linked together. The failure of any one of us represents the failure of all. To complete the relay successfully, each of us must be committed to contribute our best in our own unique way. It takes quality time to implement and perfect a mental training program. It requires a systematic approach and a high level of commitment; but the rewards are substantial. Take the baton and run with it!

REFERENCES

Higgins, A. (1979). The principles of running, jumping and throwing. In R. Munro (Ed), *Run, jump, throw: Elementary orientation handbook.* Ottawa: Canadian Track and Field Association.

Orlick, T. (1986). *Psyching for sport: Mental training for athletes.* Champaign, IL: Leisure Press.

Orlick, T. (1980). *In pursuit of excellence.* Champaign, IL: Human Kinetics.